girlosophy

anthea paul

REAL GIRLS EAT

ALLEN&UNWIN

contents

Introduction

Welcome to **girlosophy – REALGIRLSEAT**. If you're a reader who's been with us for the journey so far, you will already be aware of girlosophy's survival kits for your soul and mind. In this title – the sixth book in the series – we shift the emphasis to the body and how best to support, love and honor it with food.

This is not a book about restrictive eating. In **REALGIRLSEAT** you will not find a "diet", or some eating guide for your body type that limits you to certain foods and not others. Diets are bad for your health and, if taken to extremes, dangerous, possibly even life threatening. **REALGIRLSEAT** is about finding out for yourself about which food makes you feel great, energized and ready to rock. It's about what works for you and how you can use food to look after your SELF.

This is food with heart AND soul. Food is more than just fuel for you to go out there into the world – it has a profound impact on your emotional and spiritual wellbeing. As with any other part of your life, knowing how and what to eat is all about learning to trust yourself and your choices. Let's face it, what's right for you may not be the same as what's right for someone else! But how do you work out what is right for you? Answering this question is what **girlosophy – REALGIRLSEAT** is all about.

So much has been written about dieting and cooking. In many ways too much. In this day and age how do you eat well if you don't aspire to be a world-class chef, you're too busy traveling, studying, working, building a career and just getting on with everyday life to find the time to even think much about what you're putting into your mouth? The thing is, unless you're planning to eat out every night of the week you're going to have to master the basics of cooking at the very least or you're going to starve. Let's keep things practical and as simple as possible – less is more in many ways – especially when it comes to long-winded discussions about food.

I am a pretty basic short-order cook. When I was in high school we had a book called *The Commonsense Cookery Book*. Unfortunately I no longer have a copy – I'm not even sure it's still in print – but I do recall that the simple recipes in it were actually pretty inviting and have become the basis for a lot of my cooking today. The recipes were short (and sweet!) and pretty much foolproof, as I demonstrated time and again in cooking class. I'm still not much of a chef, but I am an enthusiastic one. Although my personal road to being a "foodie" is still very much a work-in-progress,

Food truly is the nectar of the gods

SANTA VITTORIA
Fruit Nectar
PEACH
125mL

with **REALGIRLSEAT** I set out to at least stir a sense of adventure that will encourage even the most reluctant of non-kitchen hands into a little culinary exploration!

Since **girlosophy – A Soul Survival Kit** was published, many readers have written to me on the related subjects of food, health, body image and eating disorders. Sadly, for many young women (and others), food is a constant source of anxiety. There is much suffering about food that is eaten or not eaten, as the case may be. The dominance of food as a social glue contributes to our obsession with it. I am hopeful that with **REALGIRLSEAT**, a lot of the fear can be taken out of food for young women everywhere. There are no rules here, simply some ideas that will, with some luck, contribute to your overall health and enjoyment of life. I want to restore some of the balance and return the joy of eating because food truly is a gift that keeps on giving.

We all need to eat food that is fresh, nutritious and properly and, most importantly, lovingly prepared. Food should not only enable you to survive, but to thrive. This is real soul food.

RIGHT FRESH
NUTRITIOUS HEALTHFUL
ENVIRONMENTALLY
SUPPORTIVE PROPERLY
AND LOVINGLY PREPARED
FOOD=REAL SOUL FOOD

While at first the focus of **REALGIRLSEAT** may seem to be on the practical, true to Girlo form there is, as always, a spiritual underpinning. Believe it or not eating healthy and wholesome food can be one of the most spiritual activities you can do, regardless of your personal belief system, or lack thereof! Here we'll also be looking at eating in a holistic way; exploring how you can eat in a way that is not only good for your body but is good for your soul as well.

REALGIRLSEAT wants to make sure that what you eat is also good for the planet too. Fortunately for most of you who read these books, access to food is not usually the problem. As you read, each of you will be given the opportunity to consider what you might feel and how radically different your life would be if the food you may often take for granted was suddenly not available. Tragically this is the case for millions of people every day. Poverty and hunger are chronic global problems and the stats on the imbalance in food availability around the world should make each of us alarmed and ashamed. Spare a thought for those who don't even know what it's like to walk into a supermarket, let alone go shopping for anything their heart desires. Those of us who can and do owe it to each and every one of them to eat well, to eat intelligently, to not deprive or harm ourselves for fads or fashions, and certainly not to waste the precious food we are so lucky to have.

Food and its accompanying offshoot of health - body image - have ventured into difficult territory in the past two decades or so. The food and diet industries of today are massive and operate on an international scale. It's well documented and accepted that these industries and the media that supports them have drastic and far-reaching consequences on the health and self-esteem issues that confront all of us, especially young women.

Food is not (as certain media would have it) the impediment to wearing designer jeans, nor is it a barrier to the so-called "perfect" body. The challenge for all of us is to rise above such artificial imagery. I believe the best response is to "eat" oneself to physical strength, emotional wellness and spiritual balance. In nourishing yourself properly, perception and sense of reality becomes even more clear. By treating food as having the potential to generate power, strength and energy in your body, and by making considered choices, each of us can fuel up a greater and more brilliant future for the world and the generations to come.

We should all remember, or we should at least be aware, that buying food is a political act - when consumers spend, marketers, companies and industries respond. Girlosophy's prediction? Food will be THE hot topic of the millennium. Who's got the good stuff? Who will be able to afford to eat healthily in the future? Who's eating all the food now - and who's not getting their fair (and deserved) share? With the twenty-first century upon us, it is not only time these questions were put on the agenda, they must be solved.

girlosophy - **REALGIRLSEAT** is conscious eating. As with all the girlosophy books, consider it a call to action. Get equipped and seek out further information if you need to, but be aware, there is much conflicting information about food, nutrition and health out there. **REALGIRLSEAT** will show you a different perspective, namely the positive role food can play in your life. It will make you knowledgeable and help and support you to make better choices for your health, in both the short and long term. It's not about denying yourself. It's about loading up, in the best and most nutritious way possible.

Eating for one's health and for the health and wellbeing of the planet has never been more critical, nor has it been more possible than it is now. There is a good deal that can be positively done by you from this moment onwards, for a better world. As with all things, it starts with each of us as individuals.

It is my hope that you - and those connected with you - will be inspired to eat in a way that serves your mind, body and your spirit equally. I wish you the joy of experimentation with new and unusual food, the fun of cooking for yourself and those you love and - not the least - the happiness and supreme satisfaction of fullness!

Enjoy.

Anthea Paul
Avalon Beach, 2005

Nadi Markets, Fiji,
July 2003

10

I am a fussy eater. **I have to come clean with readers on this point: it's one of the reasons this book exists.** Anyone close to me is well aware of my particular preferences and quirks food-wise. It's a part of my personality. It's also the legacy of a combination of things, such as six years spent at a boarding school in my teens and years spent overseas - travel experiences left me with a few food phobias that I still occasionally struggle with. In my time too – thankfully well behind me today – I have probably been on most of the popular and hyped-up diets. Having become aware that those same diets probably did my metabolism and my body more damage than they ever did me any good, I no longer diet at all. With a good deal of hindsight I now understand I didn't need to go on a diet - ever! I thought I knew what I was trying to achieve but in reality I had absolutely no idea about how to achieve it.

JANE FONDA & LEG WARMERS

In the eighties (when I went on a diet for the first time), there were many diets and fitness regimes to choose from. There was *The Jane Fonda Workout and Diet* book, Victoria Principal's *The Body Principal*, the Pritikin Diet, The Israeli Army Diet, The Macrobiotic Diet, the Fit for Life diet and numerous other magazine diets that I can now only vaguely recall. While listing them here for the purposes of this book, I am struck by how similar these sound to The Zone, Atkins, The South Beach diet and the Raw Diet - diets that people talk about and magazines report on today. They are not necessarily all bad - indeed many people thrive on the Macrobiotic Diet - but one thing that hasn't changed is that they are tabloid-driven. Sadly, despite the chorus of warnings by health and medical professionals in recent years, little has changed in the dieting landscape in the 21st century. Adults are larger on average than ever before in history and children - from Western countries - are in the midst of an obesity epidemic. **It is clear, despite the inroads to health and nutrition in the past few decades, that in the war on fat – and the world of body image and weight – nothing has really changed at all.** Inundated and overloaded with information, we worry about calories and fat content, protein vs. carbohydrates and high or low GI. The information is often cleverly swathed in celebrity weight-loss success stories and "makeover" specials on television but it is often contradictory and has little if any relevance to how we should live and eat on a day-to-day basis. And for all the confusion one thing is certain: women everywhere are more weight obsessed and body-image conscious than ever before.

At my boarding school the meals often contained too much starch and over-cooked vegetables. There wasn't a grain of brown rice and certainly no tofu to be seen and no one I knew had ever heard of soy milk! The food dilemma was one thing but I was also over-exercising, ignoring my body's need to rest, eating too many carbohydrates for energy (I thought), and not nearly enough complex carbohydrates. Consequently, my energy would rise and fall like the stock exchange throughout the day. I also wanted to be a vegetarian – not only for philosophical but also for health reasons – but I wasn't educated enough about protein and protein substitutes or "good" fats.

I also felt tired quite a lot. **I was avoiding meat yet missing important B-group and other essential vitamins. I was not eating enough legumes, nuts and soy products – good protein substitutes – and was eating far too much dairy produce in some sort of bid to get protein and calcium.** As a result, I developed allergies and I also seemed to get colds more often than I should (even though this abated somewhat when I became a vegan in my university years). **I wasn't eating enough greens and salads,** mainly because the salads at the school were terrible but also because salad at the time was a pretty basic concoction of limp lettuce and soggy tomatoes. This is vastly different today where a healthy salad with tons of ingredients can be a meal in itself.

Like most of the girls at school, **I suspect I was fixated on food – for all the wrong reasons. I wanted to be fit and strong and slim. But this** was impossible with the way I used to go about things and with what was available to me at the time. At the end of my high school years I had "gone off" food and become listless, depressed and – for the first time in my life – I actually gained weight!

MYSAVINGGRACE in all of this was that I didn't - or rarely - ate take-away or junk food. When I was growing up, we simply didn't have the plethora of fast food outlets nor the other options for convenience eating that are so commonplace today. And in any case, I just didn't like eating it as most of the convenience foods were - as they still are today - based around animal products.

My family never ate fast food either so this was another thing in my favor. It is also the main factor that makes my experience quite different from the situation most young women face today, where fast food outlets and eating out is a large part of family life. Fast food outlets are so prominently signposted and located near public transport and at major locations that they have also become convenient meeting places for young people who are just starting to be socially active. Even without the inherently obvious wisdom of *Supersize Me* - the award-winning documentary about McDonalds that was released in 2004 (and which everyone should see) - we all know something's not right with the fast food industries and the way they do things.

It is now an accepted and scientific fact that once **fast food becomes a regular part of a lifestyle, there are almost always detrimental health consequences.**

DIETING SUCKS

I learned the hard way, that dieting (especially crash-dieting) and restrictive eating not only does you damage, it can add weight and it can destroy your health and looks.

Before I started at high school I was probably like most girls my age: healthy, happy and naturally active, ate whatever I was given at family meals and I never even thought about, let alone knew, what I actually weighed. I was actually a pretty skinny kid/teenager, with an enthusiasm for snow skiing and sailing. But everything changed dramatically for me once I started at high school. Weight became the absolute focus.

Many girls back then used to binge eat, as if they would never ever see food again, and then they would throw up after meals. We now understand this as the classic behavior associated with bulimia. Bingeing was common. Anorexia nervosa, although less common, certainly existed. Moreover, there was just a collective neurosis about eating and weight that pervaded almost every aspect of school life. And we were so young! Many of us hadn't even fully developed physically yet.

As young women, it seemed the entire world used to revolve around food, not only in terms of when we were going to get any, but what part we were actually going to eat when we did. For some, it became a badge of honor to see who could go without food for the longest or – at the other extreme – who could win the toast eating (bingeing) competition in the dining hall. Supervised meal times with senior students, special diets on application and food allowances sought to regulate things, but our eating habits were pretty much out of control. No one went to the heart of the problem and girls were left to their own devices to cope. What became a way to pass the time between weekend outings soon developed into a dangerous addiction and an obsession for more than a few. Binge eating or not eating food at all cannot solve your problems.

It doesn't make you happy and It certainly doesn't make you healthy.

15

FROM VEGETARIAN TO VEG-AQUARIAN

During my time at boarding school I still ate dairy foods. In the spirit of "I'll try anything once", when I became a student at university I thought maybe being vegan would be the answer. At the time eating vegan was a bit extreme (some would say it still is) and in fact it was quite difficult. Very few places apart from the local Hare Krishna kitchen and one other vegetarian restaurant locally provided produce and meals that were free from animal content. I was avoiding animal and, therefore, dairy foods altogether. I was determined and rigid, even to the point of drinking dandelion root coffee! But this eating plan wasn't a healthy long-term solution as I was still missing the major food groups I needed to feel well and energized. I was still missing pieces of the food group puzzle! As I was convinced it was the right thing for me, I stuck to my "regime" for years just by being picky and fussy, however not always with the results I thought I should be reaping health-wise.

In time this was phased down to a more realistic and manageable eating plan (well, for me anyway) but being vegan brought me a new appreciation for all living things. Consequently I still find it distressing the way most farm animals are treated, especially cattle, which are often raised cheek-by-jowl in commercial feed lots and are killed in appalling circumstances. The unspeakably miserable living and dying conditions of these and other animals, such as chickens and other types of poultry, should make everyone stop and think about what food choices they're making.

While I still have the same convictions, they are more moderate than before. These days I incorporate some animal foods, such as fish and very occasionally organic chicken, into my eating plan just to ensure I don't miss certain vitamins. Plenty of people thrive on a vegan or a vegetarian eating plan, however I have found that I function better on a "veg-aquarian" routine for my own health and wellbeing.

17

Before a moderate way of eating can be found, there is always the other extreme. While I was living in New York during the nineties, I somehow came full circle and went back to eating a much wider range of food, although I was still a strict vegetarian. In New York, I was living fast, eating out almost every night and going to parties and functions and well, just going hard generally. After all, it was New York and everyone was doing it! New York City had fifty types of bagels and the biggest, sweetest muffins! As I soon discovered, it couldn't go on like this forever – not for my health's sake and nor for the sake of my spirit.

I was a member of a gym and I had Central Park on my doorstep but for the first few years of living there, I struggled with fluctuating weight. The meal portions were way bigger than I was used to and there was a lot of hidden sugar, salt and fat in the food. I wasn't cooking nearly enough for myself. I learned the hard way that it's only when you cook for yourself that you know what actually goes into the meal. The cost of the fast food lifestyle takes its toll in many ways, not just physically but energetically and spiritually (not to mention financially) as well. Finally, I decided that enough was enough.

COMING FULL CIRCLE

It was time for a change.

A much-needed stint in California resulted in a thorough **overhaul of my food and exercise habits.** It also reminded me of other lifestyle-related changes, such as meditation, which I had let lapse in the busy New York social whirl. In many ways, California was the best thing that could have happened to me as it brought me to a new understanding of what can be done with **food to bring health and energy** levels to new heights.

AND BACK TO SCHOOL It took me more than twenty years to understand that what I really needed was information! I desperately needed some cold hard facts about food and nutrition. That would have been a terrific start to my understanding of the physiological changes hormones have on my body and just of understanding my body in general. It would also have given me a greater knowledge about the specific foods, crucial for total health, women need. I needed to learn about body chemistry and to gain a complete understanding of what the female body needs if it is to have lots of energy and optimal health. **How much calcium did we need and how can we get it? What sort of protein was best? Were all fats in food bad? What do we need to eat if we're doing loads of physical activity? Does food or the lack of it affect mood? (And yes, it does.)**

I needed this information when I was in my teens and I didn't get a lot of it until I was much older. But I now have a clear understanding that if we truly want to enjoy lasting health we need to get seriously equipped in the knowledge of what different foods do to and for us. I am still learning, but my jigsaw puzzle has a picture in it these days. So that's progress. I now see my individual needs against the backdrop of the smorgasbord that truly is available. The ongoing task for each of us is to keep on trying to find out more about what makes us individually run at our best.

It takes courage to begin, and it takes real perseverance to prevail, but what you gain is priceless. And it will set you free.

MY COOKING RULES

It's been quite a journey. I'm back to cooking a lot and organic natural foods as much as possible. I still change products from time to time but this is only because I am concerned about what's actually "in" the foods I put into my body. I change something if I discover something better that I can be doing. I read produce labels obsessively (the one thing I still obsess about regarding food!) and I now take careful note of the manufacturing process of anything I buy. But - and this is key - it's not a dieting thing. I no longer believe in the notion of "going on or off a diet" as I now believe we are all on one all the time. For me, it's about my personal eating plan and how and what I plan to eat to operate at my best. I don't always do what I know I should, but at least I now know what I should be doing. I have finally taken on the responsibility for my own health. My cooking rules!

MEALSONWHEELS

Because it is easy for me to drop weight when I'm working really hard or traveling, I try and eat a lot more – and I'll admit it's sometimes an intention that doesn't always translate – when I'm stressed or busy. If it looks like I might miss a meal when I'm traveling or working long hours or if I am going to make a long car journey then – as much as is reasonably possible – **I plan ahead. This way I don't end up having to eat fast or junk food on the road. I pack lots of fruit and a home-made trail mix consisting of a variety of nuts, organic raisins or dried fruit and pumpkin seeds in a zip-lock bag or Tupperware container.** Home-made sandwiches, cut into fingers, then wrapped in foil and tucked in a cooler, work well for driving/eating scenarios. I also take lots of bottled water in the car. (Remember: water, water, water!) It is not only healthy and tasty, it's cheap to eat and drink like this on the road. Not only that, you'll never even be tempted to drive through those golden arches.

To me, the important thing is whether what and how you eat is healthy for you or not. That is why I prefer to use the term "eating plan". Generally I dislike leaving things to chance with regards to my health. Not only that, when I plan meals I am more likely to maintain a balance of vitamins and to keep an eye on variety so I don't drop an essential food group or miss out on one accidentally, just because I'm busy. The (bonus) consequence of this regime is that I feel more free to have the odd "blowout", when I can enjoy a serving of ice cream or chocolate cake or some other treat.

What I am constantly doing is updating my eating plan with hopefully better foodstuffs and increasing the variety of my meals as much as possible. **I found rice noodles a few years ago, and I now use them to make my own Thai or Balinese dishes. These offset my previous reliance on wholewheat pasta, which I now use much more sparingly in my cooking. Ditto with low-salt and wheat-free products, such as Tamari soy sauce.** Substituting old outdated food habits with new good ones is a bit like updating your wardrobe. Some things should be chucked! As more organic produce becomes available and, most importantly, as I become better informed, the whole process becomes easier and even more enjoyable.

This book will hopefully provide some inspiration for you to discover what foods will work for you in the long term. There is no such thing as a diet or an eating plan that works for every person or every body. That much is clear. However, if you have been diagnosed by a medical or health professional as having a medical problem that requires you to follow a certain food plan or diet, then you should follow the advice you receive. In RGE you will not find a "diet" for your body type that limits you to eating certain foods and not others. Putting yourself on a diet or a restrictive eating plan without medical supervision or without knowing what you're doing is not just foolish, it could even be dangerous if taken to extremes. This book is not about restrictive eating in any sense. **It is about how to love and respect your body, and understand how food is its primary energy source.**

As I discovered – far too late really – there is no need to go on a diet if you are in good health and of average weight for your height, frame and age. If you are unsure what you should weigh or what the average weight for your height and age is, have a medical professional assess you. The average weight/height index is different in each country and I urge all readers to consult a professional if they have any doubts or wish to discover what is a normal range for their personal dimensions. It is important to do this on an individual basis.

Dieting when it is not needed can ruin your (normal) metabolism – the rate at which you burn calories or energy – and set you up for crazy mood swings, digestive problems and worse. I talk about this a bit more in Dieting Sucks: Part 2 (on page 30) You just need to eat well and sensibly (i.e. thoughtfully and with a bit of background knowledge), **enjoy your treats in moderation and do some regular exercise.**

As we all should know by now, some sort of physical activity on a regular basis is essential for long-term health. Walk, do yoga, jog on the beach, run with your dog, ride a bike, swim, go surfing, dance or do whatever you prefer and whatever works for you. Do it three to four times per week. And that's it. It really is that simple. You'll need a certain amount of perseverance to see which food brings you the best results and which sends your energy levels sky high. However, if you regard yourself as an ongoing personal science experiment – an experiment where you eat fresh produce and cook yourself nutritious meals – I guarantee you'll be rewarded.

As I have said in the introduction, *girlosophy – Real Girls Eat* is about learning for yourself which food makes YOU feel great, energized and ready to rock. It's about what works for you and how you can use food to look after yourself. I also hope it will encourage you to find out more about your health in general and, in the process, **enjoy more of it.**

Remember, food is the love you show your body. It's powerful stuff!

21

BECOMING PROACTIVE

As a part of keeping myself up to date, I often query local businesses about the contents of the items on their menus or the products in their stores. I can report from my own experience, it is absolutely possible to activate change if you present a good case to your local suppliers. **Once you get informed and arm yourself with a positive attitude, you'd be amazed at how you can bring about changes, even at a micro level.**

People in business are consistent in one respect at least - they all want happy customers. They also want customers who return. Once retailers understand that their customers prefer their food to be organic or free-range, in my experience they will usually do their best to provide it.

Ask your local shops whether they stock or use certified organic or antibiotic-free or hormone-free or free-range chickens and eggs, and dolphin-safe tuna or other ocean produce that hasn't resulted in the incidental deaths of inedible and/or protected marine life. **Ask if they use salt and if they use organic produce for juices.** On the other hand, if (for whatever reason) they can't or won't use such produce, you can nicely and politely explain to them that you won't be able to shop or eat there anymore and - importantly - why you won't. It's your body and your health and you should therefore **be actively concerned about what you are consuming.**

Organic Chick Peas

REALGIRLSEAT

Real girls and young women need real food for real life – that much is clear. Some magazine, advertizing and fashion models may not eat much or profess to not needing food in order to be able to do their job, or for a host of other reasons, but that's not what is healthy in the long term.

All women should know that a photograph can completely deceive. The camera does lie when it's used for certain purposes. There are lenses to make people look thinner than they are. There are certain known angles that make more – or less – of a silhouette. But the camera at certain other angles can be extremely unflattering no matter what shape the subject is. That is one reason why models are often paranoid and accordingly don't eat or eat as little as they can to still be a good "coat hanger" for the clothes they wear in photographs or on the catwalk. **No one looks that way all the time (not even the models themselves!) and it is unrealistic that anyone should aspire to look that way.**

Ask a professional athlete what she eats and it's a totally different story. These girls can't be waif-thin – they wouldn't win matches, races or tournaments. An athlete needs a lot of food to build muscles for strength and endurance. They try and eat more not less. And they are usually – if they're serious about performance – very concerned with the fuel they put into their body and would never dream of missing a meal. Most athletes have an excellent understanding of what they run on to produce their personal best. As we all should! Personally, I remain optimistic that more young women will admire the healthy physiques and eating habits of athletes rather than fashion models in the future.

If you are a real girl living life to the fullest, you need tons of energy to get what you want from your body and to maintain high levels of energy. **Treat yourself well: vow to only put fresh, wholesome food into your system.** Each person has a unique body and body chemistry though, and here's where the confusion begins. As any viewer of the popular television series *CSI: Crime Scene Investigation* can tell you, no one else has your DNA! There is nothing exactly the same about our shape or body chemistry from one person to the next. No one looks like you and you don't look like anyone else. That's why no one needs what you need, specifically, to be at your healthiest.

EALGIRLSEAT

LOVE THAT BOOTY

We can all focus on things we feel might be better about our bodies but when you criticize your body you actually feed it negativity, which is not good for you ENERGETICALLY. The way we think, feel about and feed our bodies is a pure reflection of the self-love we have ... or don't have. Anything we think is "bad" about our bodies is only because we have been fed marketing and fashion nonsense. Who dictated there is only one ideal shape that we simply must be – in order to be able to wear midriff-baring tops? An option perhaps, but certainly not the only one. View your body as the awesome machine it is. Even if you only ever say, "I respect you and I'm going to look after you the best I can", it's a lot more positive than being abusive and critical, silently and on a daily basis. Your body has a momentous task in life – it's here to help you evolve, get you where you want to go (Mount Everest, anyone?), or perhaps to have children at some stage. The point is you must start respecting it and yourself, no matter what shape you think you're in.

Respect means finding out what you need and then giving it to yourself. **Love means you affirm to yourself** and a higher power if necessary that you deserve to be having the best food and nutrition possible and that you love yourself enough to want to do that. Food is your gift of love to yourself and the first sign of respect you give your body. Deprive yourself of food and you deny your body love.

We are all walking around as engineering miracles as far as science is concerned. Your body is the most extraordinary machine you are ever likely to be in contact with. It needs to be looked after, respected and admired – by you, not necessarily by anyone else. You'll drag it all over the world and make it tolerate all kinds of things but it stays with you, trying to do you right, throughout your life. It's only fair that you return the favor! Never mind what anyone else thinks, the body wants to LIVE and it is specifically designed to survive. Before the real journey can begin, you have to LIKE yourself as you are here and now. Just doing that will bring major changes to your body! The next thing you need to do is to start LISTENING to your body. It's very good at giving clues as to what works for it and what doesn't. **Amazing things happen when you truly** LOVE **yourself as** you are.

24

bootylicious

LIKE LISTEN LOVE LIVE

TRUST YOURSELF – your intuition is your best friend

When we talk about "listening" to the body, we are really talking about two things. **In one sense there are signs your body will give you to indicate its health or otherwise energy, wellbeing and vitality or illness, lethargy and injuries.** The other is more conceptual; it is your own knowledge as to what is really good for you. Deep down we all really know what is good for us. There isn't a person alive who has demolished a whole packet of potato crisps or box of chocolates in one sitting and felt that it was a healthy thing to do! You know when you overindulge and/or when you're not giving your body what it needs and what it's asking for. That's why your intuition – your ability to listen to what is inherently truthful for your needs – is the first essential bow in your quiver of health.

INTUITION – your inner knowing – will guide you to what is right for you personally. It's there to help you, not just as the stern voice of your conscience. You need to know that you must act on it and not "talk yourself out of" the rightness of what you feel. Don't worry that you'll get out of control if you trust your instincts about what food you need. **Think of it as the friendly voice that's looking out for you, helping you to make good, positive and healthy choices.** But you need information as well, to make your intuition truly helpful to you. When you have the correct information and you use your intuition based on that, amazing things happen. You begin to take care of yourself and become fully aware of what your body needs and what it is telling you. Balance then becomes possible.

LOOKINGAFTERYOURSELF

Looking after yourself is a key theme of all the **girlosophy** books. Learning to look after yourself mentally, physically, emotionally, financially and spiritually is a huge task that requires complete commitment. As I touched on in TRUE CONFESSIONS, eating disorders are prevalent in many countries today – particularly in affluent countries – and it is adolescent girls and young women who are most at risk from developing them. Most women have either experienced one directly (whether temporary or otherwise) or at least know of someone who has.

Eating disorders can be tricky to define. Anorexia nervosa, bulimia, bingeing, extreme fasting are all eating disorders. One may share symptoms with another or be a fairly temporary precursor that, in time, might become a deepening of another, different disorder. Different phases in a sufferer's life may manifest a different type of eating disorder, making it difficult to treat. Because controlling food intake becomes the sufferer's basic expression of personal power, all eating disorders are the result of an imbalance energetically and, often, a distorted perception of the body.

Eating disorders occur when food intake, body image, self-esteem, psychological and emotional problems, peer-group pressure and weight all collide. This is why you need to wise up about the reality of these disorders and also why it's vital for everyone to get into a healthy lifestyle and eating plan.

EATING DISORDERS CAN KILL

Dieting or restricted eating when taken to extremes can bring years of medical and psychological problems not only for the sufferer, but their friends and family as well. Eating disorders are a serious medical problem and they can require hospital treatment, rehabilitation and long-term counselling for the patient. The health consequences are vast and extremely serious – memory loss, loss of menstrual cycle leading to infertility, muscle wastage, dehydration, kidney failure, liver malfunction, gastro intestinal bleeding, chronic depression, skin problems, osteoporosis (bone deterioration), neurological complications and heart failure to name just a few – and some of these can be fatal.

I encourage each reader to do his or her own research on these wide and varied symptoms. Get equipped in knowledge so you can help a friend or family member who may be hiding or not acknowledging their problem. There are many websites where you can look them up but the list of the physical symptoms at http://www.something-fishy.org/dangers/dangers.php is as extensive as it is frightening. Google "eating disorders symptoms" and check out the many online resources available.

MYRANT.com

Everyone accepts that eating disorders are a growing and extremely worrying problem, but it's also generally accepted that magazines and advertizing images are by far the main influence upon the desire of most women to be thin and therefore considered beautiful. Women buy these magazines and the products that are advertized in this manner, thus we are complicit in our own objectification. We each need to really think about this. We especially need to think about why we allow it to continue when it does such a disservice to our psychological, physical and mental wellbeing – and that of our little sisters too.

Apart from wishing the general media would stop running articles about which celebrity lost or gained weight, **I would like to question all girls – and all women – as to what they think being thin will do for them.** Many I have spoken with believe it will solve their problems, make them attractive to others (especially prospective partners), get rich and be socially popular, ultimately, be successful in life. Nothing could be further from the truth. Just because you look a certain way is no guarantee of anything. **It has no bearing on whether you are a good person or not, how intelligent you may be or whether you will find your soul mate!** Even if you have something incredible to contribute to the world – which is a much better focus – this has nothing to do with how you look. How you look physically is no barrier to having a successful life. It only matters if YOU think it matters.

The images in magazines are NOT real life. They are carefully constructed and artificially contrived scenarios, composed and produced by teams of people whose expertise lies in creating illusions that sell products. They want you to think their product will make you look like that so you'll buy more of what they are flogging ... duh. The end result? Being THIN has become synonymous VISUALLY with "having" cool stuff, "going to" cool places and "hanging out" with the cool people – in other words "being" cool. But being cool has everything to do with being an innovator – read: an individual who does things her way – and not a follower. Most magazines rely on you following their lead, so they're giving you an illusion that they are cool too! It's basically a fake reality, cleverly packaged and relentlessly presented.

The ongoing deception relies on women having low self-esteem and wanting to be in on it so they feel "worth it". Trust me, you are already worth it and no product can give that to you. You have to give it to yourself. The illusions will only continue to work with your willing participation in the deception. Once you are aware of this, you'll start to see your entire world in a different light.

THE GODDESS WITHIN
(and The Goddess Without)

The one thing that we should all take with us on our journey out into the world is that we have to treat ourselves like the Gods and Goddesses of the mythology. They were pampered and well looked after and enjoyed the hedonism of earthly delights – they had the nectar after all! When we eat, we should ensure we are giving ourselves the same beautiful energy from the available sources outside our bodies, equal to the energy we expect our bodies to bring forth in return. For our inner selves to be balanced with our outer selves, we need to understand and seriously respect this equation. Goddesses without food have no energy so there can be only a limited and a diminishing life force. To be a luminous, radiant and powerful being, with the richness of life experiences, you have to eat your way to a higher state. It's a daily task ... but it's the only way to live.

GIRLO SCOUTS ARE PREPARED FOR ANY SITUATION!

If you are prepared for things, you are less likely to be caught unaware. That might sound like basic advice, but what I'm talking about is a mixture of discipline and preparedness that will help you to make good choices. For example:

✳ It is probably not a good idea to pore over the latest fashion magazine and then immediately go to the shopping mall to buy the swimsuit or any clothing you saw in it. Go for a walk, have a light meal, drink plenty of water and then go shopping. **Shop with purpose, a sense of individual spirit – this can be hard in a mall, I know, but try anyway!** – and with a clear awareness of how you actually look in the clothes you buy – not some fantasy fed to you by the media. And remember, your wardrobe (particularly how your stomach looks in a bikini) is not the most important thing in the world. Going to the beach and enjoying the ocean and nature, on the other hand, is important!

✳ **Don't skip breakfast** and then play catch up by eating convenience foods that are high in sugar and carbohydrates for the rest of the day. These set up a cycle, sending your energy levels up – briefly – and then bringing them crashing down. Your mood will most likely swing in a similar pattern. Plan to eat as early as possible to set your day up the right way. If you want to be cool as a cucumber all day, you'll have to eat right so you stay that way.

✳ If you are going out for a social activity – concert, opening or party – where dinner is not on the evening's agenda, factor in your own pit stop – you can always re-join the group after you've eaten. Or, make sure you **eat before you go out** and give yourself plenty of time to eat without rushing. Better yet: invite everyone around to your place and cook an early dinner there first, before you go out.

✳ **Carry nuts, seeds, raisins and fruit** in a zip-lock bag in your handbag so you will always have something on hand for that moment when hunger strikes or your energy drops.

✳ **Above all, think ahead and be prepared as much as you can.**

Looking after your "Self" means training yourself to be aware of the glamorous illusions and fake set-ups presented in the media. You don't have to buy into it. If you do, it won't make you happy in the long term. You need to protect yourself! Create your own rules based on a healthy lifestyle. This will generate positive energy for you personally, which will help you in infinite ways and on every level is a powerful thing. Be positively selfish and choose your individual happiness and your personal progress instead of someone else's version.

DIETING SUCKS PART 2

30

Plan your meals to be healthy instead

If your food intake is too restrictive, if you deprive yourself of certain essential food groups or if you refuse to think about food at all, you are actually making things harder for yourself. While it can be argued that a diet is a form of an eating plan that would be missing the point! **Your body will fight back if you don't treat it well and, although you will initially seem to drop weight, over the long term it will refuse to cooperate with you.** If it doesn't receive regular and good amounts of food, the body will think it is in starvation mode and it will plan an elaborate counter-attack, which includes stashing more fat – and this translates as extra weight for you – for the low-food or "famine" that it is preparing itself for.

All the body needs is healthy food that helps it to function at a high level for you. When you understand that, once you give your body healthy, nutritious food, it will find a level of functioning that is perfect and unique for you. **It will love you back! That's why it's important to plan your meals to be healthy.** Make sure you read up about the important food groups (see page 32). Once you learn the basics, you will soon be able to take one look at something and instantly know what food group it falls into. **That way you won't miss a group and you'll make better choices all the way.**

Knowledge + **Planning** + **Commitment** = **Health**

IMPORTANT NOTE TO READERS:

The only diet I can possibly sanction or recommend at all is one that is diagnosed by a medical or health professional as being absolutely necessary for an individual's health and wellbeing. If such a diet is deemed essential then the individual's restricted eating plan should be closely and regularly supervized and monitored by that same medical or health professional. If you have not had a diagnosis by a medical professional then it is my firm opinion that **YOU SHOULD NOT BE ON A DIET** or any type of restricted eating plan, under any circumstances.

31

THE (fab) FIVE FOOD GROUPS

GROUP	TYPE OF FOOD	PER DAY	NUTRIENTS
1	BREAD CEREAL RICE PASTA	6-11 servings	carbohydrates, iron, thiamin, energy, protein, fat, fiber, magnesium, zinc, riboflavin, niacin, folate, sodium
2a	VEGETABLES LEGUMES	3-5 servings	vitamin A (beta-carotene), carbohydrates, fiber, iron, magnesium, folate, potassium
2b	FRUIT	3-5 servings	vitamin A, vitamin C, fiber, complex carbohydrates, folate
3	MEAT POULTRY FISH EGGS NUTS	2-4 servings	protein, iron, vitamin B12, zinc, niacin
4	MILK CHEESE YOGURT	2-3 servings	calcium, protein, energy, fat, cholesterol, carbohydrates, magnesium, zinc, riboflavin, Vitamin B12, sodium, potassium
5	FATS, OILS, SWEETS, SUGARS, SODA, MARGARINE	eat sparingly	calcium, protein, energy, fat, cholesterol, carbohydrates, magnesium, zinc, riboflavin, Vitamin B12, sodium, potassium

32

Note: This table is based on the American health guidelines model, and I stress, these are only guidelines.

WHAT'S IN A SERVING?

A serving varies from group to group. Here's another table to give you a rough idea:

GROUP 1
1 standard slice bread
$1/2$ cup ($3^1/_2$ oz) pasta or rice
30 g (1 oz) cereal

GROUP 2a
1 cup (1 oz) leafy (raw) vegetables
$1/2$ cup ($1^1/_2$ oz) cooked or chopped vegetables
$3/4$ cup (6 fl oz) vegetable juice

GROUP 2b
medium-sized apple, banana, orange etc
$1/2$ cup (3 oz) cooked (poached) or chopped fruit
$3/4$ cup (6 fl oz) fruit juice

GROUP 3
60-90 g (2-3 oz) of cooked meat, poultry, fish,
$1/3$-1 cup ($1^1/_2$ oz) nuts
2 eggs

GROUP 4
1 cup (8 fl oz) milk/yogurt,
30-60 g (1-2 oz) cheese

GROUP 5
medium-sized plain cake
30 g (1 oz) sugar
30 ml (1 fl oz) olive oil

KNOWLEDGE = POWER

On the left, I've listed the good stuff – the things you really need to know. To get this stuff together, I have consulted various government and nutritional websites for the current health guidelines. While the information does not vary much between Western countries, do be aware that these are "rule of thumb" guidelines for a Western or primarily European-based diet. If you are interested or want to get further specific information for your country then search the Internet. Plug in any combination of the following keywords: nutrition (and/or health); guidelines; five food groups – and specify your country.

The five food groups are normally presented as a pyramid. The bottom layer and the largest portion is the source of what should comprise the majority of one's daily food intake known as Group 1. You work your way up the pyramid to the top layer – the source of what should comprise the smallest part of one's food intake – Group 5. The nutrients and the recommended daily servings of each group are listed in the side bar.

NUTRITION and other facts of life

The basic idea is to select foods based on the food pyramid so you do not miss important components of your nutritional needs. The key is to eat a variety of foods and to balance your food intake with the physical activity you do. **Choose plenty of food from Group 2, fruit and vegetables, and only a small amount of food with high levels of fat.** Stick to the recommended servings for each group and keep your sugar, salt and sodium intake to moderate levels.

If you are not aware of them it is quite easy to miss groups of food, which means you'll be missing out on essential nutrients, vitamins and minerals. This can affect your overall levels of energy and health. It's so important to really get to understand each of the groups and what role they play in your vitality and general health.

FOODFOLKLORE
(why potatoes won't make you fat!)

It is absolute nonsense to suggest that one food by itself can make you fat. Unless it's the only food you ever eat, and/or you eat ridiculous quantities of it, it's not biochemically possible! Isolating one food group as if it has certain "weight gain" properties and is therefore "worse for you" than other foods is not the answer. **Weight gain is a complex process that doesn't happen overnight. It is a combination of consistently overeating, emotional factors, the body's particular metabolic and chemical reactions, and time.**

Granted, some foods contain more calories and therefore it's obviously more sensible to eat them sparingly – think chocolate here. As always, the answer is in the size of the portion and the way it is cooked. Sure, potatoes contain carbohydrates and starch, so the best way to eat them is in small amounts only. It is also preferable to eat them in the context of a meal. As a normal, smallish side serving with a piece of grilled (broiled) fish and a mixed salad for dinner there is nothing wrong with them. Eaten in a large quantity as a snack between meals (for example, French fries!) potatoes can certainly be high in calories and fat laden. It's not the healthiest way to eat them.

The best way to eat any food is for energy and wellbeing. If you eat with the aim of maximizing health and energy, you pretty much can't go wrong.

BLOODSUGARLEVELS One of the hot topics in health and nutrition over the past few years has been centered around blood sugar levels. Certain foods are classified as having a high **glycemic index (GI)**. This means that food gets converted into glucose in your system quicker than other, lower-rated GI products. Just as not eating any food can send your blood sugar level low (low energy), too much of high-GI foods will lead to an upward spike in your blood sugar levels (high energy) – but only temporarily. You'll come crashing down quickly. Low-GI foods don't spike as high and are more sustaining over a longer period. The extremes created by high-GI foods are not healthy. We should eat them rarely and consciously, as when eaten in large amounts it is thought that high-GI foods can lead to diabetes – which is when the body is unable to process glucose properly. **Eat regular meals of low to medium GI content so your blood sugar level doesn't swing too high or low and keeps your energy levels and brain chemistry constant.** This is definitely the way to go!

Nowadays, a lot of food products have packaging which alerts you to the GI rating of the product in question.

Label Queens

That's right girls, if you really want to be sure about what's going into the precious vehicle that is your body, you should read the label on every product you wish to buy or eat. The information is there on the packaging and it will tell you things such as:

* any added vitamins and minerals

* sodium levels

* genetically modified (GM or GE) ingredients (e.g. Olestra, some soy products) or non-genetically modified ingredients (non-GMO)

* added or no added sugar

* hydrogenated fats, man-made fats or natural oils

* preservatives added or preservative-free

* colorings and additives (e.g. monosodium glutamate – MSG)

* sugar substitutes/artificial sweeteners (i.e. aspartame)

* organic produce

* processed ingredients

* reconstituted components

* imported ingredients

* reconstituted ingredients (such as fruit)

* country of origin.

35

LYCHEES OP WATER, LICHT GEZOET
NETTO INHOUD 567 GRAM
NET WT 1–LB. 4–OZS. (567 GRAMS)

My personal rule is that if I can't pronounce the ingredient(s) or if it looks too "scientific" on the label, I shouldn't be having it at all! If you actually read all of the ingredients on some of the carbonated drinks on the market you'll notice many are chemically based or use artificial sweeteners.

I go for products that have had the least "interference" wherever possible. Once again, less is more! Use your best "squinty eyes" on everything that's on the supermarket shelf. You may be in for a bit of a shock at what's really in some of your favorite snack foods, but you'll soon know which products you can trust and are going to be the best for your health in the long run.

For many of us – and for much of the time – eating can be an emotional activity. **We eat when we are upset, anxious, happy or angry. We eat out of over-excitement, loneliness, boredom and frustration. We eat to fill up the space within ourselves creatively. We eat in order not to feel the pain of experience or the frightening intensity of our emotional capacity.** Identifying what triggers us to eat – or not to, as the case may be – at certain times more than others takes a lot of objectivity and awareness. We need to be conscious of what our emotional state is when we eat or when we feel the need to eat, and if it's not hunger-based, this could be a time when you would over-eat.

We may only have an objective view of ourselves and be aware of our emotions on the rarest of occasions. In a perfect world we all would have 20-20 vision and hindsight, but mostly we are caught up in the moment so it is impossible to step aside and see what is happening clearly. Food as emotional camouflage is a subject I dealt with in **girlosophy – *The Love Survival Kit***. Here is an edited extract from that book.

Food (f)or Love

When we are in emotional and physical balance we know what feels good to eat and how much food is enough. When our emotional needs send mixed signals to our physical body, food addictions, cravings or hunger denial can spiral out of control. **The way we feel about food and react to it affects each of us personally. What does food mean to you?**

Food is something to be experienced as a part of life. For some people eat only when they remember to – it's simply not a high priority on their list. Do you relate to that mindset or is eating an event that consumes all of your waking moments? Is food your enemy, the one thing you fear, a permanent test of your willpower and a reminder of your "weakness"? Do you believe you are a better person if you "go without", and that this somehow reflects a self-discipline and control over your body? In the West there is no lack of food, so what is lacking? **Are you craving love and using food to fill yourself up? Do you think you are worthy of love?**

Be honest with yourself. Analyze your "food craving index" and use it as a gauge of where you are emotionally. How much love do you have for yourself and for others? Do you actually believe you are lovable? When you feel the urge to eat too much or too little, try to shift the focus from your stomach to your mind: what's really going on for you right now? Are you under pressure and feeling unloved or just feeling lonely? Are you angry – at yourself, your parents, your partner? Who are you trying to punish? Who really gets punished when you don't respect your body's needs? What do you really want out of life? **Can you see the link between your attitude towards food or eating and your personal view of yourself?** These are all tough questions, but you can learn a lot about yourself by attempting to answer them honestly.

Replace obsessive thoughts of food with ideas. Express desire, don't ingest it: use your desire for food to channel your real desires. Whenever there is desire there is creativity. Whenever there is creativity there is love. And plenty of it, too.

Emotional eating goes to the heart of why some people develop obsessive behaviors and eating disorders. The reasons can often be complex and can sometimes be unraveled only with professional support in the form of a psychologist or therapist or other mental health expert. If you think you have - or if someone you know has - a problem with emotional eating or some kind of eating disorder, tell someone who can help. Parents, relatives, teachers, older siblings, your family doctor, can all provide the support you need and the first step towards getting professional help.

Energy to go (for the athletic girlo, the student, the young mum or the young executive)

If you desire optimum energy to take on the world, you're going to have to start eating like you mean it! Here are some examples of the kinds of choices you might make for a midday meal.

If you are an **ATHLETE** or participate in a lot of sporting activities, you'll need to ensure that your level of protein intake is adequate to build muscle and your carbohydrate levels are also sufficient for endurance and stamina. Our tuna pasta lunch salad (see page 132) would be an excellent lunch choice for any girlo athlete.

If you are a **STUDENT**, you need to concentrate for long hours. Nuts, leafy greens, brown rice and some sort of fish (which is "brain food"!) would be perfect as a lunch choice. You could eat the tempeh brown rice recipe on page 168 or the fish tacos recipe on page 146 would also be terrific. Sushi rolls (page 142) and the nori salad (page 130) work really well for energy and can usually be found on most campuses.

If you are a **YOUNG MOTHER,** you need to function well on limited amounts of sleep. Fresh juices (page 106) and our salad sandwich (see page 138) are fast and healthy lunchtime fare to help you cope. Your calcium intake is particularly important when you are breastfeeding so be sure to eat loads of leafy greens and dairy products or, if you are lactose-intolerant, drink calcium-enriched soy or rice milk.

For the **WORKING GIRLO**, the temptation to keep working through lunch or drink coffee with the chocolate biscuits to keep you going during that afternoon meeting is a huge one! It would be far better to try some of our couscous salad (page 134) or our Chinese chicken salad (on page 140) and, if you are really prepared – Girlo-style – you could take either one with you to work in a Tupperware container.

It's about knowing what your day might look like and what your needs may be during the different phases of your life. It doesn't have to be complicated, in fact the best things for you are often very simple. Once you click into the available choices, you'll see they are endless.

MEAL TIMES IN MANY TIME ZONES

Planning meals when you're on the run – at work, overseas, on a plane – can be a major effort at times but one well worth making. If you know you'll be traveling by plane, especially for long-haul flights, book the vegetarian meal in advance when you buy your ticket. Apart from the added bonus that you're often served first, vegetarian and dairy-free meals tend to be healthier than the normal meals served on commercial flights. They contain more salads, fruit and high-protein foods. They also contain less sugar and fat-laden stuff, which usually makes you feel bloated and lethargic when you get off at your destination (note: these foods often worsen jet lag as well).

At work you can find a local healthy place to eat and place an order to be collected at lunchtime if you are time-poor. Get to know the proprietors and explain you are trying to eat really healthily and they'll usually try to help you. You could also bring your own food to work and keep it in the fridge until you're ready to take a break. Take pieces of fruit and eat them chilled with a glass of water or fresh juice as an in-between meal booster.

If you're overseas in a country you have never been to before, it can be hard to eat well, consistently. Lonely Planet or other guides for most cities and countries have excellent and extensive reviews on a variety of restaurants, hotels and local markets where food is served and their maps will show you how to get there. The venues have usually been tried and tested by other intrepid travelers and the guides are updated constantly (make sure you get the latest edition) by independent travel-types. You'll reap the benefit of many people's experiences if you do your homework before you go. You can eat well, wherever in the world you happen to find yourself.

SHELF LIFE
– don't be blind on the date

While we are on the subject of the supermarket shelf, it's a good habit to always check the use-by date on a product. At those times when you are digging around in your cupboard for something to use in a recipe, make sure you re-check the date to ensure the product is still fresh. If it's a jar of say, sauce, where you use a little bit at a time, check the date again, each time you go to use it. **Refrigerate products that come in jars after opening** and always take leftover canned foods out of the can and store them in an airtight container or covered bowl in the fridge, for a maximum of three days. **Be aware that cooked rice contains lots of bacteria when left for a day or two and fish and all meats do not keep well after the first serving.** Be methodical and throw out old leftovers that have been in the fridge for more than 48 hours – the fading life force and increased likelihood of bacteria growth of such old food means that there's not much good they can do for you anyway!

HEALTH FOOD STORES

It may come as a surprise to some, but health food shops aren't always healthy! They do have loads of fantastic products but like any other store they also have products that aren't necessarily good for you. Check the ingredients on the labels of their products – just as you would in any other shop.

BEING A HYGIENE QUEEN IS EASY

Smart girlo chefs put as much effort into keeping their food fresh, clean and bacteria-free as they do in keeping any other area of their life in tip-top shape. This is an important part of staying well. Food poisoning can occur anywhere and one of the reasons is usually a lack of hygiene. Being a hygiene queen is an invaluable lifetime habit to cultivate!

The storage of the food you buy to eat is super important. After all, you've gone to the trouble of shopping well and thoughtfully so looking after it is only sensible in order for it to stay fresh once you've dragged it home. And so you can have total confidence when using your items, there are a couple of basic tips to follow.

The first and most important rule for girlo chefs is to wash your hands thoroughly with warm water and soap before commencing cooking, and then again before eating, especially if you've been handling any sort of raw meat or fish.

Wash fruit and vegetables as soon as you bring them home. A small scrubbing brush is good for stone fruit and vegies as it effectively removes traces of stickers and general handling.

Store items that need refrigerating first when unpacking groceries. Remove all wrappings and packaging on seafood, poultry and meat products, place on a plate and then cover before refrigerating.

Plastic cling wrap is a useful tool, but it is plastic, which means it contains chemicals and therefore some level of toxicity. If the plastic touches the actual food, remove the piece that has been in contact with it by cutting away or tearing it off.

It may be better to place food in a ceramic bowl and cover with foil or just fit the plastic across the top so it is airtight but not touching the food.

Tupperware containers in a variety of sizes are useful, as are glass jars for storage. After use these should be put through the dishwasher or disinfected with boiling water.

If you live out of home (or even if you live at home) the share-fridge scenario is often a tough one. Clean out the fridge and wash the shelves regularly. Vanilla essence is a gorgeous homey scent that indicates you are house-proud.

Just because a product is frozen that doesn't mean it will last forever! Check the freezer contents regularly and be ruthless with things that have been there longer than one month to six weeks. That means throw them out - even ice cream goes off eventually.

The real secret of being a great chef is organization. Prepare and chop items before you start cooking and put things back in the fridge or in their containers with the lids on tight as soon as possible. This way they're not sitting out on the bench for long periods of time while you chat to a friend on the phone or whatever!

Aluminum foil is helpful for things like meat and cheese. Make sure the seal is as airtight as possible.

Clean and clear as you go. Buy packets of recycled paper towels and keep these handy for spills. Wipe down surfaces in between the preparation of different recipe stages, especially when any animal products are involved. Rinse out cloths and sponges well and place them where they can dry thoroughly.

Kitchen cloths should be fresh daily - a maximum 24 hours in the kitchen before they are due at the laundry!

At Girlo's cooking school, it's a bacteria-free zone and this means your health is safe on every level ...

SOME SCARY
TO THINK ABO

SOME SCARY FOOD
FACTS TO THINK ABOUT ...
NATURAL IS NOT ALWAYS GOOD FOR YOU!

44

Just because a label says a product is "ALL NATURAL" or "NON FAT" that doesn't mean it's necessarily good for you. It could be full of sugar and/or sodium or it may be made from genetically modified (GM) or genetically engineered (GE) products in the manufacturing process. Raw sugar that has undergone minimal processing and eaten in moderation is probably fine. Highly refined sugar on the other hand, while apparently "natural" is probably more harmful to the body. Some labels scream "NON FAT" like it is the best thing on the market but the added sodium or substitute sweetener that often is part of the fat replacement, among other things, isn't good for you either. It's better to have some real fat instead of something that's been artificially replicated.

LIFE FORCE: RIGHT ENERGY

There is a good argument to suggest that the energy in foods is dissipated by the handling, transporting and manufacturing process and consequently they're not all that good for you if carted thousands of miles. Sun is what imbues food with life force, that's why fruit and vegetables always make you feel so healthy and full of energy. Eat food that has been locally produced and has had a minimum of handling or transporting. Visit grower's markets and buy local produce to ensure the food you use in your cooking has as much freshness and is as energetically powerful as possible.

FOOD FACTS

Go for the real thing every time.

GM products are arguably produced naturally. But what are genetically engineered and modified foods? Are they good for you or not?

Genetic engineering – n.
Scientific alteration of the structure of genetic material in a living organism. It involves the production and ... the use of various methods to manipulate the DNA (genetic material) of cells to change hereditary traits or produce biological products.
The American Heritage® Dictionary of the English Language, Fourth Edition, Houghton Mifflin Company, 2004.

And: "... plants that are resistant to diseases, insects, and herbicides, that yield fruit or vegetables with desired qualities, or that produce toxins that act as pesticides."
The Columbia Electronic Encyclopedia, 6th edition, Columbia University Press, 2003.

Both these and more information about the genetic engineering of food can be found at:
www.answers.com

It's a big question and the answers are not always clear cut. Governments and biotechnology companies say there's nothing wrong with GM food and produce; however, I would caution everyone against eating such food regularly or – if possible – at all. We still do not know the effects these foods can have on our bodies in the long term. The technology that produces such food is still relatively new.

Be aware that GE or GM food is controversial. Recently, the government of Zambia refused millions of tonnes of food from the United States in famine aid because the food was genetically engineered. Other countries such as Zimbabwe, Mozambique and India have refused aid in the form of GM foods, as they too have been worried it would set a precedent for other countries to "dump" their lower-grade and/or high-risk produce on them. In addition they did not want the GM seeds to infiltrate and pollute their pure and long-standing agriculture system.

"We will stand together in preventing our continent from being contaminated by genetically engineered crops, as a responsibility to our future generation."
African Civil Society Groups at *The Earth Summit* held in Johannesburg, South Africa, in 2002.

GM foods are scary enough, but I'm not particularly keen on other products that fail to specify what they contain on the label either. I am hesitant to use or buy some imported products as they may not be required to add food labels by law – unlike other countries such as Australia. Say, for example, the fruit is listed as coming from a region in South America but the actual product is produced in Italy or somewhere in Eastern Europe – this is all before the product is shipped to Asia! How can we be sure what's in it? Anything "reconstituted" is a bit dodgy to me as we also don't know the kinds of pesticides used in the agriculture process in other countries not to mention what happens during the manufacturing process. And then there's the whole transport thing ... As I live on one side of the world anyway, there's just too much distance and handling and too little info on some overseas products for my liking.

45

PRESERVATIVES WON'T PRESERVE YOU!

Preservatives and chemical additives are health destroying. They may preserve the food so it lasts longer on the supermarket shelf, but they won't necessarily preserve you. It has been suggested that too many additives and preservatives from the foods we eat create cellular imbalance within our bodies. Some added colorings and preservatives have been linked with certain cancers and many are thought to cause the body to age. Basically, our bodies simply can't be a rubbish tip without some sort of biochemical fallout! As consumers we should all be aware of the real contents in the products we are eating.

46

OILS AIN'T OILS EITHER
– why real butter is better

Hydrogenated fats and oils are used in processed foods and there are indications these could cause long-term eye problems, including blindness. This is fairly recent research and it may be wise to avoid products as far as possible that use margarine, corn oil, safflower oil and man-made oils such as olestra. These are usually found in things like bought cookies, chocolate bars and other manufactured processed and packaged foods such as sweets and desserts. Oils may not be oils and that's why girlo 'chefs don't fake it! Use extra virgin olive oil and real butter in your cooking. Used in moderation and very occasionally these oils are better than any unnatural or man-made oil. If the olive oil or the butter comes from a farm that practices organic farming techniques, that's a bonus. Butter tastes better too! I stress, though, go easy on it. You don't need a free ski jump of the stuff!

SOY, WHAT?!

Soy products have really been in the spotlight in the past few years. Ever since it was discovered that the Japanese have the longest life expectancy, and that this longevity was in part due to their soy-based diet, the humble soybean has had a remarkable transformation. It has emerged to become a hot and hip commodity on the world agriculture stage. Regular (non-GM) soy milk has all the nutrients of cow's milk without the lactose, saturated fat and cholesterol. Research has even shown that soybean protein is equivalent in quality to the protein found in beef, milk and egg white. **Soybeans contain loads of iron and calcium and fiber and are low in saturated fat. Another bonus is that soy contains no cholesterol.** In addition (and this is the really good news!) soy beans contain polyunsaturated and omega-3 fats, which are beneficial in lowering cholesterol. However, as with many things in the world of food, there is controversy with soy as well. Sigh. Soy is now used in many products as a general filler (e.g. lecithin). Once again, the best advice is to check the labels on all your products and apply the moderation principle.

Soy is found in many products including: Miso/soy blend breads and cereals/soy cheese and milk/soy flour soy meats (there are even soy sausages!)/soy sauce/soy chips tempeh/tofu, and tofu desserts (soy ice cream and soy yogurt).

Soy is a terrific protein alternative to animal protein sources and is a great way to cut down on animal fats if not eliminate them altogether. Be sure to source organic, non-GM soy products and enjoy the benefits of this positive protein.

A QUICK NOTE ABOUT DAIRY vs. DAIRY-FREE:

Because of the importance of calcium for healthy bones and development, there has been a huge emphasis placed on eating lots of dairy food. Conventionally produced dairy foods (milk, cream, yogurt etc.) cannot always be tolerated by all people and cow's milk has been linked to eczema and allergies (and apparently even bed-wetting in children). In fact, dairy food in particular has been associated with a variety of gynaecological problems in women. Reducing the amount of dairy foods you consume and or substituting them with organic versions often has positive effects on health, particularly for women. And don't forget your dark leafy greens, such as spinach and broccoli, which are another fantastic source of calcium to help you in reducing your reliance on dairy foods.

RAWSTUFF

When it comes to food, fresh is definitely best and preferably it's not over-packaged and it's organic. What is organic? Well, if you Google the words "ORGANIC FOOD" this is what you get:

Definitions of Organic Food on the web:

Technically, anything that contains at least one atom of carbon. In common usage, "organic" refers to foods cultivated and processed without fertilizers, insecticides, artificial coloring, artificial flavorings, or additives. www.nutribase.com/cookingt.shtml

Food that is produced without pesticides, fertilizers, growth hormones, antibiotics, artificial additives, food coloring, ionizing radiation, and is not genetically modified in any way. www.geodsudbury.org/FoodShed/glossary.html

That seems to be a good starting point! When you juice organic fruits and vegetables, you know you will be drinking something that is way more healthy than that packaged juice, sitting in the fridge at the local corner shop - the one with a ton of additives and preservatives listed on the label. The raw stuff - in other words the fruit or vegetable itself - is what gives a juice or food its energy and its nutrition, that's why it pays your body massive dividends when you eat this type of produce.

There is also a lot of talk these days about eating as much raw food as possible. The reasoning goes that food in its original unprocessed state (and even cooking is a form of processing) is thought to be much healthier as the processing depletes the produce of its nutrition. In some ways I agree with this, however, there is something beautiful that happens energetically to you when you eat a well-prepared home-cooked meal, especially when it's made with love. You just feel better! Raw foods are good but this can be taken to extremes. Once again the golden rule applies: moderation is best.

48

Difference!"

Green Bag™

I don't own a microwave oven. Some people can't believe it when they come to my home and I don't have one in my kitchen. I always laugh when they ask me in their practically horrified tone: "But how do you live?" My answer is always the same: quite easily.

Around 90 per cent of homes in Western countries have a microwave oven, so my situation is by far the exception to the general rule. I took the decision not to have one in my kitchen on the basis that any process of heating that involves the re-arrangement of the basic molecular structure of food, I'm not too keen on. I don't want my food that fast as it turns out! I have even sworn off frozen food except in an emergency situation.

There is now a lot of research that suggests microwave cooking changes the nutrients in food. A further study monitored the changes that took place in people's blood samples after they'd eaten food heated in microwave ovens and it indicated damage and degeneration to the human body.

As is always the case with such things, we each need to decide what we personally feel about this information. **My compromise is to not worry if I occasionally have food that has been in a microwave – and to enjoy my food regardless.** I try to keep this type of heating process to the barest minimum. In other words, I am aware and I prefer not to eat food that is microwave heated if I have the choice. But, I still like to live somewhat normally!

Having said that, we should probably not be heating our food in the microwave using plastic containers of any sort. Plastic releases toxins when it is heated to high levels. Use glass, Corning Ware or other types of ceramic containers instead – especially don't use the common fast food plastic containers. Use a ceramic plate or bowl but if there is plastic wrap on top the food should NOT come into contact with the plastic. **Use the microwave sparingly, and with care.**

THE BOTTOM LINE ...

Granted, you can't always know or tell whether the food you are eating (especially if you are traveling or if you eat out a lot) is organic, contains preservatives or whether it is comprised of GM ingredients. You can't always know whether what you have ordered is heated up via the use of a microwave or not. Unfortunately it is impossible to know what products vendors use. In the quest for having some sort of a normal existence there has to be a certain amount of acceptance that you can't always know for sure what you are eating if you didn't prepare it yourself. And the thing is this: in moderation it's all probably OK! A little knowledge is helpful and I've included the above information for your personal reference and benefit. However, there is absolutely no sense in becoming paranoid as a result of knowing about this stuff and therefore not eating anything! It's better to eat the food that's available (even if it has been heated in a microwave oven) than to not eat anything at all. The health consequences of not eating are far more damaging.

49

We should assume that we are all, more than likely, eating this kind of stuff at least some of the time and so we should try not to bring it into our home cooking. **Be vigilant, choose carefully and above all eat as well as you can, as often as you can.**

Vitamins. Multi-vitamins. Health supplements. Tinctures. Protein powders. Tablets. This is the age of the pill and today it's become an accepted part of life. Sometimes it seems as though there is a pill for every occasion! Many people still wish for a pill they could take that contained the magic "cure-all" for illness and to provide them with perfect energy. However, as we've been discussing, eating natural wholefoods for energy, wellbeing ("wellness"), maximum/optimum performance and an enhanced life is what it's all about. As we've also seen, much of our so-called "natural" produce is made under somewhat suspect conditions and is of dubious or, at the very least, un-provable quality. This means that even if we follow the fab five food groups religiously, eat regular meals and "do everything right" we could still end up lacking certain essential vitamins and minerals. Therefore we may not be as healthy as we deserve to be!

I have given the topic of supplements much thought. Having consulted **medical and health practitioners (or their published work)** on this subject, I have come to the conclusion that **all women who are of menstruating age** and older who aren't getting all the vitamins and minerals they need should be supplementing their food plan with a multi-vitamin at the least.

WATERWATERWATER – the real elixir of life

Certain cola and soda drinks are BAD for you even if they only have two calories. Quite apart from the preservatives and other health-destroying ingredients they contain, they simply do not have the life-sustaining and energetic benefits of pure water. Water is proven to be the best thirst quencher, no matter what some "sports" and so-called "water-replenishing" drinks manufacturers claim. Go for the real thing instead of the expensive imitations and hydrate properly at a cellular level.

Get lots of water into your system, preferably filtered, and do try to drink at least 1 to 2 liters (64 fl oz) daily. Drink more water if you are participating in sport or other physical activities, if it's a particularly hot day, you are traveling or even if you are under stress (if you are studying for your exams or if you are busy at work). Drink more especially if you are ill.

Take a big bottle with you wherever you go and sip away, all day.
Water is the real elixir of life and the guardian of your life force.

WATER

I urge all readers to consult with their doctor or a health professional to be recommended a more comprehensive individualized program of supplements. Such a program must be designed for each person's specific needs. If you can't do that then try to find a good multi-vitamin that is designed for women. Take it with food, preferably at breakfast time.

That will really help you to go, girl.

51

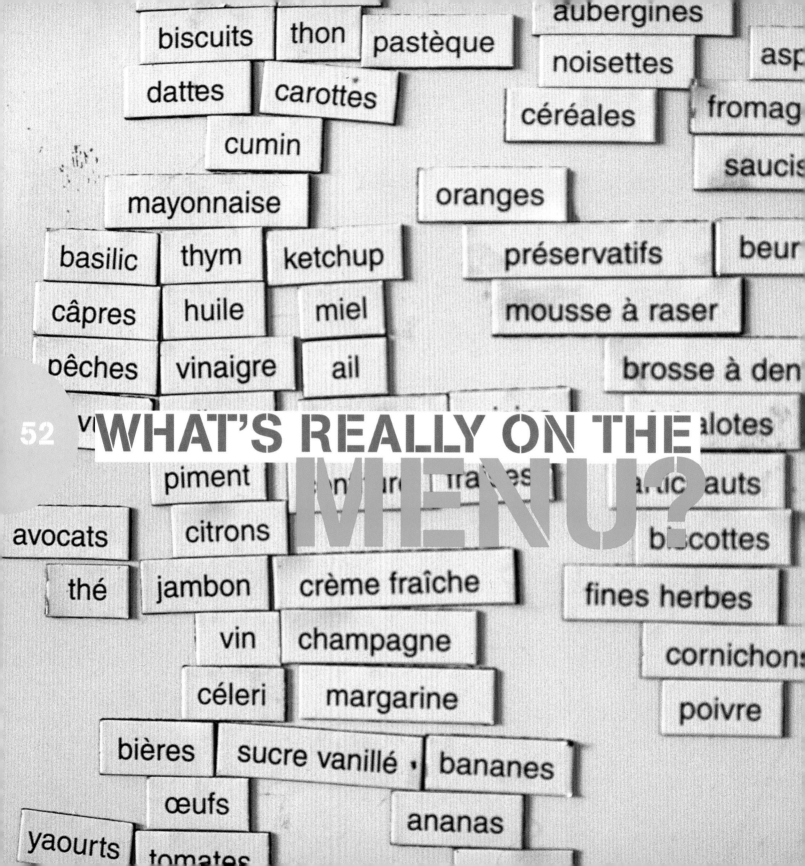

WHAT'S REALLY ON THE MENU?

FOOD and DIS-EASE or why you should never eat at the restaurant next door to a high-profile fast food outlet ...

We have already touched on the hygiene aspects of food but what about the situation where you can't control this aspect? Without creating a certain amount of paranoia, you should not eat just anywhere or just anything. Be smart about your choices. Take care when selecting a place to eat at. Before you commit, ask yourself: Does it look clean? For example, are the tablecloths fresh? Is the glassware clean and shiny? Have they wiped down the table without you having to ask? Does the kitchen (if you can see it) look clean and organized? Is the restaurant or food outlet busy? The busier the better as this means the food is turning over more and it is more likely to be fresh. If a place looks quiet I tend to avoid eating there as the food may not be as fresh if the turnover is not high. This is a rule I especially adhere to when traveling. I can't know about all the places in the world I'm going to eat at but I always scroll through my mental checklist before I commit to an establishment for a meal. As much as possible, I go on the energy and the feel of a place. So far so good, as I have only ever had an upset stomach once while I have been away in all the years I've been traveling.

If I travel I try to eat local fare. I always try to keep in mind the relevant geographic aspects of the available food. Certain restaurants will offer every cuisine and variation of food under the sun to get you to eat there! Extensive menus aside, it's probably not a great idea to eat seafood pasta in the middle of a desert in India when the locals are eating lentil curry with boiled rice. It's a good rule to remember the old saying, "When in Rome [or India, New York, Bali] ..." In other words, be shrewd and do what the locals do.

WHAT'S REALLY ON THE MENU? Eating out healthily is always a challenge. The good news is that today there are more restaurants that recognize the growing awareness - and desire - of people to eat healthily. No matter what type of food outlet you are planning to eat in though, you should always read a menu carefully when ordering and ask lots of questions from the person taking your order. You can get dressings on the side and most good restaurants are more than happy to oblige if you want to substitute or delete certain items in a dish. Ask for soy milk if you prefer it to dairy-produced milk. Ask them for olive oil to dip bread in instead of margarine, if that's what's on offer. Ask for your vegetables to be steamed instead of wok fried if that's what you feel would be best for you. Find out what sort of produce is used in a dish if you can - without being a nightmare customer, please! Be patient if you do request changes though - the kitchen may need a little more time to get your order exactly right. Remember to be discreet with your inquiries and always be polite. The person who is serving you may not know if something can be done and is probably not the person making the decisions anyway so don't take it out on them if they can't help you.

Restaurants are like people – there are infinite varieties. Wherever you go you will face choices. You don't have to order the crayfish (crawfish) or lobster that are crawling all over each other in the tank at the front of the restaurant. You don't even have to eat there in the first place! If you get stuck, you can't go too far wrong with any kind of salad or steamed or roasted vegetables. A fruit salad with sorbet ice cream for dessert is a staple on restaurant menus. My personal tip – for when you are really having a problem finding something healthy to eat on a menu – is to check out the kids' menu. Kids tend to want to eat more basic food and it's often less fat-laden. Sometimes you'll find on it simple, healthy meals that work better for you energy-wise.

VARIETY IS THE SPICE OF LIFE

This section is for those girlo goddesses who love to go around the world in ate-y ways! Those with the travel bug know that food is the cornerstone of different cultures. For real girls who live to travel, there is one truism: you will always come up against something inedible that makes you nearly throw up. **It could be the yak butter tea your kind and gracious Nepalese hosts offer you on arrival at their guesthouse in Kathmandu.** It may be the odd-looking, contents unknown stew in a neighborly English pub, which the owners are offering free with the accommodation for the night. Don't freak out! This is part of traveling. Sometimes, to be a part of the experience and to be "present", you simply have to throw all the rules out and just go for it. Far better to drink something and create a warm reception (and melt a few cultural barriers in the process) than be a boring old stick in the mud.

Be open to the variety and the richness of food on offer on this planet. It's what travel is all about – having new experiences. Getting into the food of a culture is key to understanding the people and relating to them. As our cool real girl, Petrina Edge, says in girlosophy – **REAL GIRLS' STORIES,** "Traveling . . . gave me some new things to think about. Learning and understanding new and different cultures, for instance. Food is such a big part of how we do that."

55

YOU ARE BEING SERVED!

How do you judge portions when you're in a strange house or a strange town for that matter? **Portions are personal!** Some people prefer to have small portions on a plate and then go back for seconds. Others prefer to load up only what they are going to eat. Yet others put more on the plate than they know they're going to need and then leave some. **If you are eating out, at someone's home or in another country (at an Indian wedding banquet with thirty-three courses on the menu, for instance) you need some sort of handle on what amount of food works for you.**

I visualize how much food would fit into one of those classic medium-sized take-away containers (note: they are truly international). As a general rule, I try and stick to that amount when eating a meal. Check out how much pad Thai noodles actually fit into one of them when you tip it out onto a plate. If fits a lot! I have found – through trial and many an error – that if there is any more food than this amount, I'm probably going to eat more than I need.

TAKE-OUT INTERNATIONAL INC.

Restaurants, family meals, parties, traveling ... the sheer variety of eating situations means that to eat for maximum nutrition, you always have to be "en guard!" How to eat – even when there's nothing in the fridge – is a problem everyone faces at some point and it means you have to be creative. Don't end up eating food that doesn't serve you energetically. Take-away foods and home delivery present solutions to this situation, and they can still be healthy. A few girlo tips:

✳ Choose foods that are Asian-based. As a general rule, these tend to be lower in fat and higher in complex carbohydrates and other goodies.

✳ Japanese food is always delicious and for the most part low in fat – but hold the tempura! Sushi, sashimi and maki rule.

✳ Thai food has delicious vegetable, chili, basil and rice noodle dishes that are tasty and healthy.

✳ Indian food is fabulous for vegetarians with its lentil, chickpea and vegetable recipes. Saffron rice is sheer heaven.

✳ Take-away pizza is everyone's favorite indulgence but, please, choose the gourmet type if possible: thin crust, goat's cheese, tomato and vegetarian toppings are best. Order an Italian salad while you're at it.

BLOWOUTRULES
Fries and pizza eaten occasionally won't kill you.
(Obviously not all at once please!)

The great thing about a massive pizza spree/television night with the girls is that you really appreciate it when you do have it. You know it's a rare treat, so just relax and enjoy it for what it is - occasional and therefore not the norm.

Being able to eat properly all the time when you live with friends, attend boarding school or college, live with your family or live with your significant other is not always easy. People don't necessarily want or need the same food and at the same time. You can individualize your eating plan, but to be a happy member of a happy household, you will no doubt have to make occasional compromises food-wise. You should see these compromises as one of the side effects of not always having to provide the food every single time! If you live on your own you'll have to make the effort to always have the food you need on hand at the time you need it. It's up to you - and you alone - to fill your cupboards and your fridge with food to eat. **That's why the meal that your mother or flatmate has spent hours preparing should be eaten graciously - even if you don't really necessarily feel like the meal that's been provided.**

Having said that, it doesn't mean that you always have to agree with the "food fascism" that can be a feature of peer groups. You don't have to go along with other people's choices. That goes for whether it's a group of your friends or your family!

You can still respect the choices of others, yet choose an alternative that is right for you. If your body wants or needs something healthier than fried chicken wings, you should honor that feeling.

Standing apart and being difficult isn't the way. Be the team leader and encourage everyone to order food that will be better for all of you.

ANIMALS R US

Earlier in this book, I talked about my vegetarianism. In the past I have struggled to be a vegetarian and remain healthy but it can be done. **Many people follow a strict vegetarian eating plan and have no health problems whatsoever.** Being a vegetarian means you never eat animal flesh. Vegan means eating no food with any animal products whatsoever. **It all comes down to the individual preference.**

Are you a vegetarian or a carnivore? Or are you not quite sure? Got a foot in each camp perhaps? Don't worry, you are not alone! There is a new alternative: veg-aquarian. The only animal flesh you eat is fish. Again the choices are many.

I believe that vegetarianism as an ethical philosophy and as a way of life is absolutely correct. So does practicing Hare Krishna and committed vegetarian, real girl Radha Melis. As Radha says in *girlosophy – REAL GIRLS' STORIES*: "I believe we all have souls and so we all have the right to live". The Hare Krishna movement is firmly against taking the life of any living creature, as is the Buddhist philosophy and religion. Both these compassion-based philosophies believe strongly in the rights of animals. **They regard animals as creatures who have as equal a right to life as humans.** This belief is underscored by their equally strong belief in the notion of karma – what you do today affects you in this life and in any future lives you may have.

PETA (People for the Ethical Treatment of Animals), Animal Liberation, the RSPCA (The Royal Society for the Prevention of Cruelty to Animals), AWL (The Animal Welfare League) and a host of other international furry friend support groups all campaign for correct, caring treatment of animals. I support their work and I urge all readers to be informed about the issues. For a start, watch the movie *Babe*, about the sweet little pig who goes on an adventure. Seeing this might be enough to put you off eating any more pork! I also urge you to seek out more information about corporate food (branded food). Often the branded food companies don't want you to know certain things about the foods they're selling. Sometimes the truth is often hidden in far-flung farms, abattoirs and massive food-processing plants, where no one can see. Are you sure you want to support their methods by consuming their products? Be aware and think hard about these things – it's important for the future of the planet.

There are many reasons to be grateful for the food we can so easily purchase. But we should bear in mind the world hunger problem and the poverty, which prevents so many from being able to eat. Every day, thousands of men, women and children are dying from hunger and the effects of chronic malnutrition somewhere in the world. If you have access to this book, the chances are you will never know this kind of extreme deprivation and hunger, nor this kind of existence. Tragically – and unbelievably – hunger is still a part of daily life for millions in the 21st century. Food (and water) continue **to be the major issues for the long-term** survival of many on this planet.

61

FEEDING TIME
– but turn off the television please!

"Real life is deep and complex and slowly developed and it has its roots in fundamental things. And you cannot experience those fundamental things or true pleasure in life, without taking your time." Edith Wharton, as found on http://blogs.salon.com/0001764/2005/01/01.html

Take your time. Eating should not be squeezed in between a million other activities, nor should your food just be bolted down. Sit down when you eat a meal or any sort of food. Eating time is time well spent – it's time you have taken for your SELF. Turn the television OFF. **A meal time should be sacred time. You don't need noise taking your mind away from the important things your body may be telling you while you are eating.**

Set the table properly. Knives, forks, napkins, fresh glasses of water and placemats or a clean table cloth for the table will brighten any meal and encourage everyone to get together and spend some quality time as a group. **If you're not eating with a clan of people, set yourself a pretty table anyway. It's an excellent habit to get into.**

Make the effort to create the right ambience where you and anyone who eats with you can enjoy and savor wholesome, nutritious food. Your digestion will be better, your sense of satisfaction greater and your health will benefit. Most importantly, your relationships will benefit. Have a laugh together and share the events of your lives. **Your intentions and your communications make the food powerful, energetically enhancing and positive for you on all levels: emotional, physical and spiritual. This is the real food for your soul.**

63

The point of REAL GIRLS EAT is to urge you to **enjoy your food** in whatever form it takes. At the same time, it is also to help you to understand how food nourishes you energetically, depending on the origins of the food, who made it, how it has been handled and processed etc. Apart from choosing the best food available to you in the first place, you can imbue the food you are about to eat with sacred energy yourself.

Certain **rituals before eating** can be helpful. Just giving gratitude that you have food to eat can be helpful. Say a silent prayer of thanks – good old "Grace" is powerful and positive. Or make an affirmation of gratitude with the conscious belief that the food will nourish you and benefit your body. These rituals help your body make the most of the food you give it. This is truly food for thought. **You communicate with your body every time you eat so make the experience a good one!**

Caramel Icing

1 cup firmly packed
Brown Sugar

1/4 cup of milk

Table spoon Butter
Vanilla

1/2 teaspoon
coffe escence

Cake   1/2 cup
1/4 lb   shortening   1/2 200gms
1 cup   sugar   2 cups
3/4 cup milk   1/2 milk
2 eggs   4 eggs
juice 1/2 orange   Table spoon coco
1 cup S.R. flour   2 SR Flour
1 extra cup of flour 2 Flour
                              Table spoon
                              out of flour
Cream butter and sugar. Mix in
all other ingredients for approx 5 mins
till creamy add extra cup of flour
Put in greased tin. Bake for 20
mins or till properly cooked.
     12 mins for small cakes
doubled mixte makes 6 doz small
cakes   Oven 300

GIRLO'SGOTGREATTASTE!

Take-away food and restaurant food can be some of life's true pleasures; however, most people do ultimately prefer their own cooking! One of the things you will experience through making your own home-cooked meals is that the food really tastes better. It is an inexplicable and yet undeniable fact that the food you make with fresh produce at home – and with love and positive energy – will not only taste better it is actually healthier for you. It's my belief that the whole way food is created and handled from its origins to how it is ultimately combined in our kitchens, imbues it energetically with either the positive imprint that is conducive to radiant good health, or otherwise.

In this section a baker's dozen of our girlosophers cook their favorite recipes. Savory, sweet, simple – these Real Girls cook up a storm just for you.

We have presented their plate set-ups to maximize ambience and your enjoyment of making the meal. We didn't take forever to set up the dishes as the images of the recipes are not meant to be intimidating. Don't overly concern yourself with creating a dish that looks "perfect". That would be missing the point! The recipes are presented in such a way to inspire you and give some clue as to how they can look, if you want them to! Bring your own creativity to the table and just relax the whole process. The main thing is to have a go and enjoy the result – whatever it may turn out to be!

If you don't own any crockery or have a proper dinner service or if your mother won't let you use hers, don't worry. Serve up your recipes on a supermarket plate or/with a paper napkin if that's all you've got. We own almost all of the plates you see in these pages but many came from the local Op Shop and St Vinny's. You should be able to put some edge and personality into your cooking without spending a bomb. Low budget or no budget at all? No problem. Girlo shows you how to enhance the eating experience for even the simplest occasion.

Whether eating for one or with the whole team or family, there are unlimited ways to make each occasion memorable. International and on location, we have thought up some practical, cool and casually stylish settings and ideas for Real Girls who want to savor every minute of life.

REAL GIRLS COOK

WHO: EMILIA PERRY
LIVES: NORTH SHORE, HAWAII
SURFER / WAITRESS
AGE: 24

67¢

68

I'm making Asian Burritos. They're so simple and easy, also they're really healthy and filling. I saw this in a book of recipes from Hawaii but I changed lots of the ingredients around to how I love it. Food is awesome. It gives me the energy I need to surf big waves and helps me focus on what I am doing. When I eat healthily I feel great! I love to cook and I love changing recipes here and there depending on what is in my fridge.

EMILIA'S ASIAN
BURRITO
MIX

69

"My best tip – for when you start out making them – is not to put too much in or you can't wrap the burrito and then everything falls out. Little bits work! And besides, you can always have another one. They're like little presents."

Ingredients

FILLING
Chicken/fish/tofu pieces and teriyaki sauce or butter/olive oil, to taste
2-3 cloves garlic, peeled and finely chopped
bean sprouts, to taste
2 carrots, cut finely and vertically (julienned)
1 avocado, sliced (plain or mixed with garlic and chili to taste)
1 small bunch green onions, julienned
handful of coriander (cilantro) leaves, finely chopped

DIPPING SAUCES (2)
1 tablespoon peanuts/cashews/almonds
2 tablespoons sweet chili sauce
2 tablespoons Tamari (wheat-free organic soy sauce)

NOODLES & WRAP
1-2 cups thin Asian rice noodles
1 pack round rice wrapping sheets

How to make it

Chopping: I like to put all the ingredients in little bowls as I go and arrange them all on a tray. This makes the feast look generous and you can always put what's left over in individual zip-lock plastic bags for later. I try and cut everything vertically and finely as it makes it easier to wrap things up later!

To cook the salmon or tuna, chicken or tofu: Marinate them in a few tablespoons of teriyaki sauce with or without chopped garlic for about half an hour. Then I cook them (separately) in a small frying pan with a tiny amount of olive oil in the case of tofu and tempeh pieces, or in the case of tuna or salmon pieces, I grill (broil) them quickly under a hot griller (broiler).

For the dipping sauces: I finely chop the nuts and add them to the sweet chili sauce in one bowl and then I put some plain Tamari in another bowl.

For the rice noodles: I tend to do these last so I can watch them cook, which only takes about 2 minutes once the water has boiled. You have to be careful not to overcook them otherwise they just become a gluggy, sticky clump and you can't separate a small amount for each of the wraps. Take 'em out quickly!

For the rice wraps: Fill a big bowl with warm water - not too warm or the wraps get too soggy and then you can't wrap them! This is the key to wrapping success. The fun bit starts once the rice wraps are thoroughly wet. You place them flat on your plate and start piling up all the ingredients. Wrap into little parcels ready for dipping in your choice of sauce.

*wrap, dip and eat ...
they are sooooo good!*

I'm making Porra Antequerana. It's delicious and simple to make and cooking it makes me feel like a local. It is like a thicker version of gazpacho, which I also love for the tomato, olive oil and garlic flavors. However, Porra Antequerana is far more versatile as it can be used as a dip.

Food is not just about eating – it's about preparing and sharing meals. It's about meeting up with friends – chatting and laughing over a freshly baked chocolate cake. I love trying new things and ingredients. Food can tell you so much about a place – the produce that thrives in certain areas, even the history of a small town.

JESS'S **PORRA**
ANTEQUERANA

RG
02

WHO: JESS MADDEN
STUDENT COMMUNICATIONS & SPANISH
LIVES: MALAGA, SPAIN
AGE: 22

Ingredients

1 kg (2 lb) tomatoes
6 bread rolls (day old)
1 or 2 cloves garlic
$1/2$ red or green capsicum
(bell pepper)
$1/2$ cup olive oil
salt
3 or 4 drops vinegar
50 g (2 oz) tuna or ham
1 egg, boiled
milk or water to soak the
bread in

How to make it

1. Run blunt side of a knife across the whole surface of each tomato, applying pressure to loosen skin in preparation for peeling.

2. Now using the sharp side, cut the top off the tomatoes and peel off the skin in strips (loosened by the pressure applied with the blunt edge of the knife). Place peeled tomatoes in a bowl.

3. Squeeze each tomato until all the insides are out and you are left with the flesh of the tomatoes. Discard tomato innards (or keep them to use in a tomato sauce for pasta).

4. Take the bread rolls and remove the outer shell or crust. Soak the crumbs in the milk or water for 2-3 minutes and then squeeze out the liquid and add to the tomatoes.

5. Add chopped capsicum and garlic to the bowl. Add a little salt and vinegar.

6. Take a hand-held blender and mix slowly, adding oil in a thin and constant stream. Combine until a smooth and thick consistency is achieved and all the ingredients are pulverized.

7. Take the boiled egg and dice it finely. Serve mixture in a bowl and garnish with diced egg and tuna in the center of the bowl.

74

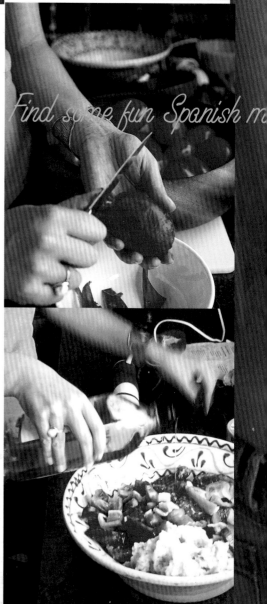

Find some fun Spanish m

Tip: Even avid garlic fans should be careful of overdoing it. Uncooked garlic has an intense flavor, and this will increase if you are preparing the dish in advance.

listen to as you are preparing it to get you in the mood!

RG 02

WHO: JONI CAMINOS
LIVES: HAWAII, USA
ANTHROPOLOGY STUDENT / WAITRESS
/ RETAIL MANAGER / TRAVELER
AGE: 24

I love food and I'm always hungry! I'm from a Chinese, Hawaiian, Filipino and Spanish background and I enjoy Hawaiian, Italian, Japanese, Chinese and Mexican food. I tend to eat whatever I want as long as it's in moderation. If I feel I ate too much junk food, I'll make up for it by going surfing or dancing hula.

I'm making Vegetable pizza. Pizza is one of my favorite foods. It's also easy to cook, fun to make with friends, and tastes good. I learnt how to make it from my step-mom.

VEGETARIAN PIZZA

ALWAYS CHECK UP ON THE PIZZA WHILE IT'S BAKING BECAUSE DIFFERENT OVENS COOK FASTER THAN OTHERS.

Ingredients

pasta sauce
pre-made pizza crust
zucchini
red onion
mushrooms
olives
tomatos
capsicums (bell peppers)
shredded cheese
Italian seasoning
garlic salt

How to make it

1: Spread pasta sauce all over pizza crust.
2: Chop the vegetables and spread them evenly
over the pasta sauce. 3: Sprinkle the shredded
cheese evenly over the vegetables so that it will
hold the vegetables together. 4: Sprinkle over
some Italian seasoning and garlic salt to your
taste over the pizza. 5: Bake the pizza on a
lightly oiled pizza pan or cookie sheet at 230°C
(450°F) for about 10-12 mintues.

TIP *Simply
choose your favorite
vegetables and
experiment with it.*

I love food and I'm always hungry!

My favorite quote on life:

"Don't ever be too lazy or too afraid of change to ever stretch your wings and live your dreams."

I'm making a really yummy beef lasagna — it's really easy to do and tastes delicious! My mother taught me to make it.

I love food! I think you should feel free to eat whatever you want when it suits you provided you don't eat too much at once and remember to incorporate fruit and vegetables as well.

Ingredients

For the meat sauce:

500 g (16 oz) premium mince (ground) beef
1 small onion, finely chopped
6 small mushrooms, chopped
1 teaspoon crushed garlic
500 ml (16 fl oz) tomato coulis (or a tomato-based pasta sauce)

For the cheese sauce:

2 cups (16 fl oz) milk
2 cups (8 oz) sifted plain (all-purpose) flour
1 teaspoon crushed garlic
1 cup (4 oz) grated tasty (cheddar or jack) cheese

For the lasagna:

1 packet lasagne sheets
$^1/_2$ cup (2 oz) grated tasty (cheddar or jack) cheese

WHO: GRETA STOJANOVIC
LIVES: TAMARAMA, SYDNEY
CURRENTLY DOING A BACHELOR OF
MUSIC ... ONE DAY I WOULD LIKE
TO WRITE AND PRODUCE MY OWN SONGS
AGE: 20

RG
04

GRETA'S
LASAGNA

81

I think anyone can have a great relationship with food provided they eat it in moderation.

How to make it

Preheat oven to 180°C (350°F).

To make the meat sauce:

1. Put some olive oil in a large pan, add the minced (ground) meat and cook on high heat until it's browned.

2. Lower to a medium heat and add chopped onion, mushrooms and garlic.

3. Pour in tomato coulis and stir for 2 minutes then allow to simmer on a low heat.

To make the cheese sauce:

1. Warm milk in a large saucepan.

2. Beat in flour, 1 large tablespoon at a time, being careful not to allow the sauce to become clumpy (a hand-held mixer is a good idea). Stop adding flour once sauce has a custard-like texture.

3. Add garlic and cheese and continue to beat until consistent.

Putting it all together:

1. Get a large baking dish (sheet), approx 30 cm x 20 cm (12 inches x 8 inches). Place a layer of the meat sauce in the baking dish.

2. Next add a layer of cheese sauce (don't worry if the two layers slightly mix together). Then add a layer of pasta sheets - these may be broken to fit appropriate size of dish.

3. Repeat the layering process until dish is full and there is a layer of cheese sauce at the top.

4. Sprinkle a thin layer of grated cheese on top.

5. Place in oven and cook for 45 minutes or until the top cheese layer is golden brown.

82

83

DON'T PUT TOO MUCH SHREDDED CHEESE ON THE TOP OR IT WILL GET TOO OILY AND WON'T TURN A NICE BROWN COLOR.

I'm making Balinese Coconut Pancakes.

My Dad, who is Balinese, taught me this recipe when I was about ten years old. They are a traditional dish for the temple festivals and dances in Bali (Indonesia). They are meant to be green normally because the Balinese put food coloring in them, but everyone gets a bit freaked out if you do that here! They are a bit of a treat and they remind me of when I was little.

I like planning out what I eat. I eat junk food too, but I know how to pull it back if I've gone too far ... the healthiest thing I do for myself is eats lots of vegetables and I drink milk for calcium.

HANNAH'S **COCONUT PANCAKES**

WHO: HANNAH TAUFAN
LIVES: NEWPORT, SYDNEY
HIGH SCHOOL STUDENT / CHICKEN SHOP ASSISTANT
AGE: 16

85

Ingredients

desiccated (unsweetened shredded) coconut
pure palm sugar (buy this in a pack)
organic plain (all-purpose) flour
milk
eggs
olive oil

Tip: Be careful not to burn the coconut and the sugar! Keep a really low heat (simmer) and watch it carefully.

How to make it

To make the coconut and palm sugar filling:

200 g (6^1/$_2$ oz) desiccated (unsweetened shredded) coconut
250 g (8 oz) palm sugar (usually it's about half a pack)
2 cups (16 fl oz) water

Soak the coconut in the water in a saucepan for about 15 minutes. Chop up the palm sugar and add it to the mix over a medium heat on the stove top. Leave simmering.

To make the pancakes:

2 eggs
2 cups (10 oz) organic unbleached flour
1 cup (8 fl oz) milk (or half coconut milk, half normal milk)

Mix these together in a bowl until creamy, smooth consistency, but not too runny! Basically, you pour the pancake mix into the frying pan when it's hot (but not too hot: it shouldn't burn the oil) and you just pick up the pan and make the mix run all around the rim of the bottom of the pan. Once it's cooking and browning underneath (you can check this by lifting one side partially with a spatula or egg slide) - and when you have courage or before it burns - flip it! I like to do it in the pan with no hands, but you have to be willing to have a few disasters with this method. It's more fun though.

Put the pancake on the plate and place a couple of spoonfuls of the coconut/palm sugar mix in the middle. Wrap and roll into hand-sized parcels. Eat!

"Whenever I do the first one, it's always a mess, so it's 'Bye, Bye' and into the bin ... I'm a messy girl!"

I'm making Banana Loaf.

My mum taught me this recipe and the great thing about it is that it's really yummy but you don't feel as though you're stuffing your face with rubbish when you eat it. Mum is definitely a fantastic cook – she's also very inventive! I am a real "foodie" sort of person – ever since I was a kid I have loved my food a lot. And I enjoy my food without worrying too much.

88

SOPHIE'S BANANA LOAF

RG
06

WHO: SOPHIE WELDON
LIVES: CLAREVILLE, SYDNEY
HIGH SCHOOL STUDENT/
DRAMA STUDENT/ ACTIVIST
AGE: 15

89

I believe in healthy eating, not "stopping" eating! I won't not eat to lose weight.

We never have soft drinks in the fridge, we always have lots of fruit. My mum believes in variety. I am a conscious eater – I plan my meals. I have a big breakfast before I go anywhere and I take nuts and things to school to keep my energy going so I can concentrate. That's really important to me.

Ingredients

125 g (4 oz) unsalted butter
1 cup (8 oz) sugar
3-4 drops pure vanilla essence
2 eggs (free-range please!)
1 cup mashed ripe banana
250 g (8 oz) plain (all-purpose)
wholemeal (wholewheat) flour, preferably
organic, unbleached
1 teaspoon baking soda
1 teaspoon ground sea salt
1 teaspoon ground cinnamon
$1/4$ teaspoon ground allspice
1 cup (8 fl oz) milk containing 1
teaspoon of lemon juice

I love this quote by Oliver Wendell Holmes:
**"A mind once stretched by a new idea
never regains its original dimensions."**

How to make it

Preheat oven to 180°C (350°F).

You need a mixer (well it's easier if you use one but if you don't have one then use a wooden spoon and some wrist action plus arm muscle!) to mix the butter and sugar until lightly creamed. Add the vanilla to the bowl, then add the eggs and banana. Then, grease the cake pan. We have a loaf-shaped pan and Mum showed me how to line it with the paper from the butter wrapping. You can just grease it with actual butter, though, if your butter doesn't have the paper.

Hot tip: **If you use unsalted butter, add a teaspoon of salt to the dry mix.**

In a separate bowl, combine the dry ingredients: flour, baking soda, salt, cinnamon and allspice. Then, add this dry mixture slowly to the mixing bowl with the butter mixture, and keep mixing on medium speed, adding the milk with the lemon juice a little at a time, mixing as you go.

Once it's thoroughly mixed through, pour or spoon the mixture into the prepared cake pan. Bang the loaf on the table a few times to get rid of the air bubbles in the mixture! Place in the oven and bake for 45 minutes. Also if you want to eat faster, spoon exactly the same recipe into a muffin tray - muffins only need 25 minutes to bake.

At 40 minutes, check the oven and if you want to, place a couple of chocolate squares along the center of the cake. Close the oven door again and leave for a final 5 minutes. Take out, leave in the pan for another 10w minutes and then using a knife to clear the sides, tip the loaf out onto a cake wire to cool slightly before serving. Warm cake is the best! Serve with a cup of tea. Truly yummy.

91

WHO: MARIANA IGLESIAS
LIVES: MATRAVILLE, SYDNEY
FINE ARTS STUDENT
AGE: 18

92

I'm making Cheese and Bacon Omelette. It's quick, easy and yummy. My mum taught me to make it one day when I was in primary school. So after I learnt how to make it, it became my after-school tradition (it still is!). I love food. I come from a Uruguayan family which means you eat and eat and eat! My mum is constantly cooking these great family meals, that you just can't say no to.

MARIANA'S OMELETTE

How to make it

1. Chop all your ingredients (Parsley, bacon and garlic).

2. Place in a bowl, with 2 eggs, ½ cup of milk, a sprinkle of salt, pepper and nutmeg and mix.

3. Heat pan, spreading butter or margarine around the whole pan.

4. Pour the mix, making sure all the contents are scooped out and spread evenly in the pan.

5. Once most of the mix is cooked on top place a large plate over the pan, flip your omelette onto the plate, then slide it back in the pan, to cook on the other side.

6. Once cooked, serve on a plate and sprinkle some chopped parsley.

Eat and enjoy!

Ingredients

2 eggs (for each person eating)
1 cup (8 fl oz) full milk
garlic paste
fresh or dry parsley
butter (for the pan)
2 rashes bacon
shredded cheese

Make sure to butter around the edges of your pan or else you'll

When cooking remember to make sure that the mixture is evenly spread around the pan.

95

be left with a sticky mess!

WHO: KATE SHERRIFF
LIVES: PADDINGTON, SYDNEY
OFFICE MANAGER/RECEPTIONIST: PR
AGE: 19

96

Note There's a _____ learnt
when cutting the _____ during a commercial _____ality and
although I haven't quite _____ of cooking, it
certainly helped me to _____ speed and precision.

I'm making a pasta dish with green prawns (shrimp) drenched in onion and garlic and mixed with a tomato base served on a bed of spinach. It's great hangover food and it's not too heavy. I learnt it in Drama class: Improvization.

Food's a necessity but I eat a lot of unnecessary things! We're definitely compatible ... but then again, I think food is friends with everyone.

You may decide not to use garlic in the dish. Although you'll be eating it you'll also be wearing it for the next day or so ... in other words you'll stink of garlic so don't go around kissing anyone!

How to make it

Preparation:
1. Cut onion and garlic into fine slices. (Use a chopping board and sharp knife for this).
2. Separate and discard the shell and legs of the prawns (shrimp) from the flesh if not already done so.
3. Get a large stainless steel saucepan and fill 3/4 of it with cold water. Put this over the stove and bring water to the boil. (Add in a pinch of salt as this helps to cook faster and also adds flavor).
4. Place a second medium-sized saucepan over a medium heat and glaze the bottom of the saucepan with a small amount of olive oil.

Cooking:
1. Place the olive oil, onion and garlic into the saucepan and use a wooden spoon to gently stir it around. Make sure you don't burn the onions and garlic. Allow to cook until slightly golden.
2. Now add the prawns and season them with the pre-cooked onions and garlic.
3. Once the water in the saucepan has boiled, put in the pasta. (I use angel hair pasta which cooks in about 2 minutes)! You will need to be multi-tasked for this bit now: you have to monitor the cooking of the prawns and also the pasta. Put a timer on for 2-3 minutes for the pasta so you can focus on the prawns.
4. Add a generous amount of tomato puree (sauce) into the saucepan and mix it around with the prawns, onions and garlic. You will know when the prawns are ready as the flesh will turn from a greyish black to an orange/pink and the tomato sauce just needs to be gently heated.
5. Add spinach. Stir until leaves are wilted.

Serving:
1. Once the prawns and pasta are both cooked, remove from the heat and turn off the gas/hotplate.
2. Put a sieve under the tap in the kitchen sink and tip the pasta from the pot into it. Run the pasta under hot water to drain away the excess starch.
3. Get a large serving bowl and use tongs to distribute the pasta into the bowl and then add the prawn and tomato dressing.
4. You have now completed the recipe. Bon apetit!

Ingredients

1 onion
1 clove garlic
250 g (8 oz) green prawns (shrimp)
1 packet angel hair pasta (or thin spaghetti)
1 bottle tomato puree (sauce)
olive oil
salt & pepper, to taste
1 bag baby spinach leaves

Bon apetit!

99

WHO: NEETA LAMBA
LIVES: SARATOGA, AUSTRALIA
HIGH SCHOOL STUDENT
AGE: 13

100

I'm making a vegetable and rice dish from India called "Rice Palau". It is also sometimes called vegetable briyani. My grandmother taught me to make it. I've just learned how to do this! Every year she comes out from Delhi, India and I learn something new each time. She also taught me to make French toast! Food is great. My parents have two restaurants so I'm always around food. The food we eat is always home-made because my dad is a chef! Dad makes food for us specially and it's the best! It's what I'm used to. Learning to cook is a great skill.

Cooking for yourself means you won't have to always buy ready-made food. You have options. It's a part of looking after yourself!

Ingredients

1 onion, sliced
4 teaspoons olive oil
1 carrot, grated
1 head broccoli, chopped
1 cup (6 oz) green peas
salt, to taste
2 teaspoons cumin seeds
2 tablespoons tomato paste
5 cups (40 fl oz) water
2 cups (14 oz) rice, soaked for half an hour

How to make it

1. In a large pan, on medium heat, fry the onion in olive oil until light pink.

2. Add all the prepared vegetables to the pan.

3. Add salt, cumin seeds and tomato paste.

4. Stir for a few minutes and then cover for about 1 minute.

5. Lower heat and cover pan to allow to simmer.

6. When the vegetables are half cooked, put the water in a saucepan and bring to the boil.

7. Once the water is boiling, add the rice.

8. Once the water and rice boil, cover and leave on low heat for 2 minutes.

9. After 2 minutes stir it again. Test the rice with your fingers to see if it has softened.

10. Turn off the flame but keep it covered – the rice is then ready!

11. Combine the rice and vegetables and mix well. Serve immediately. This recipe serves between 2-4 people.

Be yourself. Whenever you see
your friends have money - even if
you don't have any - be happy!
Never cheat in life. It won't get
you anywhere.

103

Hot tip: **We used leftover vegies
from the fridge. Look at your fridge
and find new things!**

Girlo's tried and trusted recipes and great food ideas 24-7 – even when you think you've got nothing in the fridge! This section contains real recipes from the girlo crew ...

Our girlo chef, Kate Paul, has tested all our basic and healthy recipes that are within everyone's capabilities. The recipes are designed to get you started and they contain plenty of hints and substitution ideas to give you maximum opportunity to practice your skills. The "Tips" section of each recipe details some key shortcuts and hints to make your cooking foolproof ... or at the very least you'll be able to call yourself a real girlo chef! The shopping list shows you what's essential and what's optional for each recipe to help you decide what you can get away with. This will help on those nights when you come home to an empty fridge or cupboard. We know how frustrating it can be when you want to make something but are missing one ingredient ... so now you can work out if it's crucial! And the "Tools" section gives you the drill about what equipment is needed to make the recipe. Sometimes it's all in the knife, or the colander ...

While we don't expect that you'll never need to look up another cookbook, we do hope these healthy and basic recipes give you a few ideas for more experimentation. You should enjoy cooking up your personal storm of treats. But remember to clean up as you go as it is less work in the long run. Girlo knows from personal experience that the mess in the kitchen is much harder to clear on a full stomach. You'll also be more motivated for a big cook-up generally if you get into this habit. Avoid the dread of the aftermath by avoiding the mess in the first place. And have plenty of clean cloths on hand so all your guests can help with the washing up!

The Green Clean is a good one if you have a tummy upset.

High-Energy Juices

Juicing is an absolute must in girlo's kitchen. We love the instant energy lift and the crazy amounts of vitamins in fresh juices. With fresh juice, the rule is to drink it as soon as it's ready so all the goodies can be absorbed in pristine condition - but sip it slowly.

Green Clean – the detoxer
* celery (top and tail)
* grapes
* pineapple (remove husk and skin)

This juice is great for cleaning out the lower intestines - it's like an internal broom. The sweet grapes will give you energy while your digestive system gets its mini-workout.

Tools:
a good juicer (these can be expensive, but are an excellent investment)
a strong, sharp knife
cutting board
peeler

DRINK YOUR GREENS!

There are so many juicing recipes, it is impossible to list every combination. What we can recommend is that you can make virtually any juice to your personal taste by working out how much you need of each ingredient. Boost your **immune system** by using particular combinations for your daily needs. Drinking fresh juices is one of the greatest things you can do to **energize your body** on an ongoing basis. Get into the dark greens: broccoli, spinach, watercress and sprouts. These contain incredible amounts of vitamins and are easily absorbed by the body in juice form. **Drink your greens and you'll feel the energy lift.**

Minty Melon – the refresher
* watermelon (remove skin, leave seeds)
* mint (add a small amount, say what can fit in a third of your palm)

Watermelon contains B-complex vitamins as well as vitamin C, making this a great healthy boosting juice.

hot tip **Add ginger, parsley and sprouts to any vegetable juice or to a carrot-apple-celery mix.**

The Power Classic is great when you have a cold or flu.

The Power Classic – vitamins C & A

* carrots (top and tail)
* red apples (de-stalk and roughly chop, leave the seeds in, they contain vitamins)

Red apples contain creatine – the great muscle building amino acid! Creatine is in many artificially produced muscle-building powders that weight-lifters use. Why not go straight to the source – the natural source that is! Carrots contain beta-carotene and other fabulous anti-oxidants.

108

Cold tip:
Freeze fruit
(especially
berries) so the
flavor you crave
is always on hand
even if it's out
of season.

SMOOTHIES
Here are three yummy drinks that are as fast to produce as they are good for you. If you are running late or have no time to cook, these smoothies will fill the hole until you get to the shops or have time to make something healthy to eat. Smoothies can get you out of a jam! We tend to use non-dairy, calcium-enriched soy milk as the base for these smoothie recipes, but it's up to you if you want to add yogurt or use any other dairy products instead. Bring your creative best to the task though: these recipes are only basic guidelines. **Ultimately smoothies can be whatever you want them to be.**

Tools:
blender (ice crushing variety preferred)
tall glass or glasses
knife & cutting board

Banana Passionfruit Smoothie
A good banana smoothie is like an old friend - always timely and consistent. Serves: 2 people (tall glasses) or 1 person if you're super hungry!

Shopping list:
* 1 large or 2 small bananas (the smaller tropical sugar bananas have the most flavor)
* 1-2 passionfruits, depending on size and juiciness
* 1½ cups (12 fl oz) soy milk
* 1-3 drops vanilla essence
* 3-4 ice cubes

How to make it:
1. Chill the soy milk in the fridge overnight.
2. Slice up the banana and put pieces in the blender.
3. Halve the passionfruit(s) and scoop seeds and fruit into the blender.
4. Add in the soy milk.
5. Drop in a few drops vanilla essence.
6. Add in ice cubes.
7. Switch blender to high and blend until mixed.
8. Serve in tall glass/es.

110

Coconut Papaya Lassi
Girlo goes troppo for our health's sake if nothing else! Here is a smoothie with more than a hint of the Caribbean about it. Jamaica anyone? All you need after having this drink is a hammock by the ocean ... Serves: 1 person

Shopping list:
* half a small- to medium-sized papaya
* 1 lime
* 1 can light coconut milk
* 2 teaspoons honey
* 3-4 ice cubes
* raw almonds shaved or chopped super-fine, for garnish

How to make it:
1. Open the can of coconut milk and pour into a glass jug and cover with plastic wrap. Leave in the fridge overnight.
2. De-seed the papaya.
3. Cut the lime into quarters and squeeze liberally over the papaya.
4. Roughly cut the papaya into small pieces and put into the blender.
5. Add the chilled coconut milk.
6. Add the honey and ice cubes.
7. Switch blender to high and blend until mixed through.
8. Pour into a tall glass, garnish with chopped or shaved almonds.

If you can't find light coconut milk, use full-cream coconut milk and dilute with water to taste. Try and use raw organic honey that has not been heat treated.

Tools:
blender (ice
crushing variety
preferred)
tall glass or
glasses
knife & cutting
board

111

Blue Berry Smoothie
You haven't lived
if you've never had a berry smoothie. This
"blue" smoothie helps you load up on your
vitamin C and fill your tummy at the same
time. Berry delicious.
Serves: 1-2 people

Shopping list:
* 1/3 punnet (tub) blackberries
* 1/3 punnet (tub) strawberries
* 1/3 punnet (tub) blueberries
* soy milk
* 2-3 chunks soft tofu*
* 2 teaspoons honey
* 3-4 ice cubes

How to make it:
1 Chill soy milk and berries overnight.
2 Place berries, milk, tofu, honey and
ice cubes in blender.
3 Blend on high until smooth.
4 Pour into tall glass/es and serve
immediately.

*Tofu is optional but it
is a great way to add some
protein.

Porridge with Apples, Pears & Crispy Walnuts

Fiber, fiber, fiber! Many a ski race – and other races we're sure – have been won on a tummy-full of porridge. It's just the greatest brekkie in winter! We like to call ours the winter fruit salsa ... warm up and go get 'em.

Serves: 2 people

Tools:
saucepan
frying pan
1 baking dish (sheet) or cookie pan
measuring cups/spoons
knife & cutting board

Shopping list:
* 1 egg white
* 1 teaspoon sugar (any kind, but soft brown sugar is best)
* ¼ cup (1 oz) walnuts
* 2 cups (5 oz) oats
* 4 cups (32 fl oz) water
* 1 cup (8 fl oz) milk – soy, normal or skim works just as well
* 1 tablespoon butter
* ½ lemon, zested & juiced
* 1 seasonal apple, peeled & cored
* 1 pear, peeled & cored
* ¼ teaspoon grated ginger

How to make it:

1 Preheat oven to 200°C (400°F). Place your breakfast bowls at the back of the top of the stove to warm from the heat of the oven.

2 Whip the egg white with a fork. Once frothy, add the sugar. Toss the walnuts into the mix, place on the baking dish and into the oven for 10-15 minutes until crunchy. Remove from oven, then roughly chop and set aside.

3 Place the oats in a small saucepan with the milk and water, and gently cook until the oats are softened. If needed, add more water or milk, to taste. It should not be dry, just soft and floating within the saucepan. Remove from heat.

4 Melt the butter in a frying pan and add the lemon juice and zest.

5 Meanwhile, dice the apple and pear into chunks – any shape or size works just fine. Add to the butter mixture as soon as you cut it so the fruit doesn't go brown. Then add ginger.

6 Stir gently until softened. Spoon porridge into the bowls and put the apple and pear mixture over the top. Serve with extra warmed milk.

Go mad with dried fruits for another topping!

Hot Tips!

Any hard fruit from winter works well with this dish, as does rhubarb and the like. You can substitute oats with other breakfast grains you prefer. You'll find these at wholefood stores or the "natural" aisle of the supermarket.

Nectarines, plums, apricots, quinces, apples and pears all work well in this poaching liquid. For the apples, quinces and pears, peel them, then add some lemon juice and zest to the mix to stop them turning brown.

Other grains such as quinoa or couscous would also be lovely under the peach.

yum!

Peachy Rice Soup

for breakfast! This dish is just as comforting in the summer as the winter – when you can substitute with winter fruit such as pears, quince, apples, etc. Serves: 2 people

Tools:

two saucepans
measure cups/spoons
knife & cutting board

Shopping list:

* poach liquid
* 1 cup (8 fl oz) water
* $1/2$ cup (4 fl oz) mirin
* 1 tablespoon real vanilla extract, check the label – it will be without alcohol
* 1 tablespoon soft brown sugar or raw sugar
* 1 orange, zested & juiced
* 1 ripe peach, dried gently
* $1/3$ cup ($3^1/4$ oz) brown rice, precooked according to the packet directions
* $1/3$ cup (1 oz) barley, cooked according to the packet directions
* $2/3$ cup (5 fl oz) soy milk
* honey or maple syrup, to drizzle (optional)

How to make it:

1 Place all the poaching liquid ingredients in a "non-reactive" saucepan. This means it should not be made of aluminum, which can react with some of these ingredients and cause them to discolor or turn them bad during the cooking process.

2 Heat the liquid gently, stirring until all the ingredients are combined and the sugar has melted. Place the peach in the cooking liquid and let simmer, uncovered, for about 15 minutes. Turn off the heat and let the peach sit in the liquid until cool enough to handle. Take out the peach and reheat the poaching liquid and boil it down to one third of the volume, keep warm at the back of the stove.

3 Make a cut around the peach like an equator. Pull apart the two halves from the pit. Gently peel off the skin – it should feel very soft, but still have a slight firmness to it – and keep the peach halves warm in the poaching liquid.

4 Meanwhile, mix the rice and barley in the second saucepan. Add the soy milk and warm up gently, stirring so it doesn't stick. When warmed through, spoon into two plates and place the peach halves on top. Drizzle some of the poaching liquid over the top and if you like, some honey or maple syrup. But try it natural first!

Home-made Muesli

Bircher muesli makes me go weak at the knees. I am definitely a museli girl! Dr Bircher-Benner's Swiss miracle has been the sustainer of many a mover and shaker on the planet, so here's girlo's version ... enjoy the gorgeous taste and feel amazing to boot. Serves 1-7 people!

Tools:
large mixing bowl
2 kg (64 oz) jar with tight sealing lid or Tupperware container
tongs & spoon

Shopping list:
* 2 cups (6 oz) puffed rice
* 2 cups (6 oz) wild oats
* 1 cup (4 oz) desiccated (unsweetened shredded) coconut
* $1/4$ cup (1 oz) phyto soy mix (made up of ground linseed, sunflower kernels, ground almonds)
* $1/4$ cup (1 oz) each of pecans, cashews, pepitas & walnuts
* $1/4$ cup ($1 1/4$ oz) each of: dried cranberries, raisins, currants, apricots, pineapple, strawberries, mango (diced), pear (diced) & figs (roughly chopped)

How to make it:

1 Mix together the rice, coconut and oats (or any other grains you prefer).

2 Roughly chop the phyto soy mix and cut down any large pieces of the fruit into small chunks.

3 Using tongs and a spoon, mix and swirl all the ingredients together so that they are evenly distributed throughout the muesli.

4 Spoon into a clean jar (even if it's new, you should wipe it out) or into the Tupperware container, and seal tightly.

You should serve about 250-315 g (8-10 oz) per bowl (1 cup plus a little bit extra!) Poached or fresh fruit can also be added. Keep your museli fresh for longer: store it in a cool place like your pantry, or even in the fridge if you are living in a really hot climate.

116

Hot tip:
If you really aspire to be a gourmet chef, you can lightly toast the desiccated (unsweetened shredded) coconut in the oven, using a baking dish (sheet).

When serving, we love to eat it with non-fat goat's or soy yogurt on the side.

117

NOTE we used all organic ingredients, easily available from your local health food store — subtract or add fruit or grains (e.g. bran or flaxseed or wheatgerm) as you like. Try to buy dried fruit that hasn't been processed with added sugars and radiated or chemically dried using sulphur — check the label! If you're still unsure, check with the health food store.

HOT TIP: *For a gorgeously tropical look — for those girlo chefs who are dreaming of the South Pacific — skewers or small shell-topped toothpicks etc. can be found at party stores, but these are optional.*

Fruit Chunks with Basil & Lime Syrup

This is a fresh way to eat your fruit serving for the day. It's also a top way to start the morning. This recipe rocks! Serves 4-6, depending on how hungry you – or the masses in your household – really are

Tools:
measure cups/spoons
knife & cutting board
small saucepan
juicer

Shopping list:
- 1 pineapple
- 1 rockmelon (cantaloupe)
- 1 papaya
- $1/2$ medium-sized watermelon
- 1 punnet (tub) strawberries
- 2 tablespoons brown rice syrup
- 2 limes, zested into strips and juiced
- $1/4$ cup (2 fl oz) water
- 1 bunch basil

How to make it:

1 Peel and de-seed all the large fruit, and cut into similar-sized chunks, about 3 cm ($1^1/4$ inch) squares (bite-sized). Leave the strawberries whole, but take off the green tops.

3 Gently cook the lime juice, water and the syrup together in a saucepan. When warm, add half the basil leaves and steep for 10 minutes. Mulch the leaves slightly with a wooden spoon. This is called "muddling"! Strain out the basil leaves and add the lime zest strips.

4 Roll up the remaining basil leaves like a bedroll, and slice finely ("chiffonade"). Reserve for the top as a garnish.

5 At this point, you can either place all the bite-sized fruit pieces in one big bowl or you can assemble them onto small skewers in any order, but ending with a strawberry. Once in their serving bowl or on the serving platter, pour the basil-lime syrup over and top with the basil chiffonade.

Mint works well in place of basil and oranges or lemons instead of limes. If you don't have brown rice syrup, **you can use honey** or sugar.

Fried Egg Sandwich

A great breakfast and one of the healthier ways to cook it! Serves: 1 person

Tools

non-stick frying pan
spatula
knife & cutting board

Shopping list:

* 1 large organic brown egg
* 1 piece sliced bread
* 1 tablespoon olive oil, butter or non-stick oil spray
* salt & pepper, for seasoning

How to make it:

1. On a gentle (low) flame, heat the frying pan while you prepare the bread.

2. Cut a circle in the center of the bread almost to the crusts. Save the cut out bit for a top.

3. Heat the oil or butter, or spray the pan, and let it heat for 30 seconds.

4. Turn up the flame to medium and place the bread in the pan and crack the egg right into the hole. You can cook the "top" next to the bread.

5. Keep the flame at medium – not high, because you don't want the bread to burn before the egg is cooked on one side. After about $1^{1}/_{2}$ minutes, lift the slice gently to see if it is set underneath. Turn it over gently to cook the top of the egg. After about 30 seconds or up to another $1^{1}/_{2}$ minutes – depending on how well done you like your egg – you can gently lift and flip the egg yolk sunny side up onto your plate. Season with salt and pepper and your favorite sauce and enjoy!

Place the egg sandwich onto some baby spinach leaves dressed with lemon juice & olive oil — the heat of the bread will wilt the spinach lightly.

121

We used low-carb spelt bread, but of course you can substitute with whatever you have on hand - English muffins, brown wheat bread, classic sliced white, yeast-free sourdough etc.

French Toast Fingers

What would a breakfast be if not a little decadent occasionally? Go on, relax a little and have one of the classic breakfast treats of all time. This is what you'd call finger-licking good.

Serves: 4 people (if fewer hold over the mix till the next day!)

Tools:

small saucepan
measure cups/spoons
small dish for egg wash
non-stick frying pan
knife & cutting board
juicer
aluminum foil

Shopping list:

For strawberry sauce:
* 1 punnet (tub) strawberries
* 1/4 cup (2 fl oz) water
* 1 tablespoon sugar
* 1 teaspoon rose water

For French toast:
* 4 eggs (free-range)
* 1 orange, zested & juiced
* 1 tablespoon sugar
* 4 tablespoons butter, for cooking
* 4 slices bread, preferably complex grained bread or low-carb
* icing (confectioner's) sugar (to sprinkle on top)

How to make the strawberry sauce:

1 Slice the strawberries into thirds, place in a small non-reactive saucepan with the water, sugar and rosewater. Gently simmer for 15 minutes, but don't let the strawberries lose their shape too much.

How to make the French toast:

1 Crack the eggs into the dish, and whip with a fork. Add the orange juice, zest and sugar, then mix with the fork again.

2 Heat 2 tablespoons of the butter in the pan. Meanwhile, cut the slices of bread into four "fingers" lengthwise.

3 Lay one finger of bread in the egg mix, dredge thoroughly on both sides, and place on side plate. Repeat with the rest of the bread.

4 Place the first bread piece in the pan, and then add enough fingers to fill the pan, but do not overcrowd. Turn the heat up to medium and let the bread gently caramelize. When it has turned golden, flip over to the other side. Keep the heat to medium-low but adjust if necessary. They will burn quickly! Repeat and use the rest of the butter as needed. Keep the cooked fingers warm on a serving platter or plates at the back of the stove, covered with foil.

5 When done, ladle the strawberry sauce over the fingers and dust with icing sugar.

Try to use yeast-free spelt bread or wholegrain bread so that this treat isn't totally naughty! Any berries work well — as would other soft fruits.

123

Butter is definitely better. Real butter in
small amounts for taste is much healthier than
margarine, which contains hydrogenated fat.
In recent studies, this kind of fat was found
to adversely affect eyesight if consumed to
excess over long periods of time.

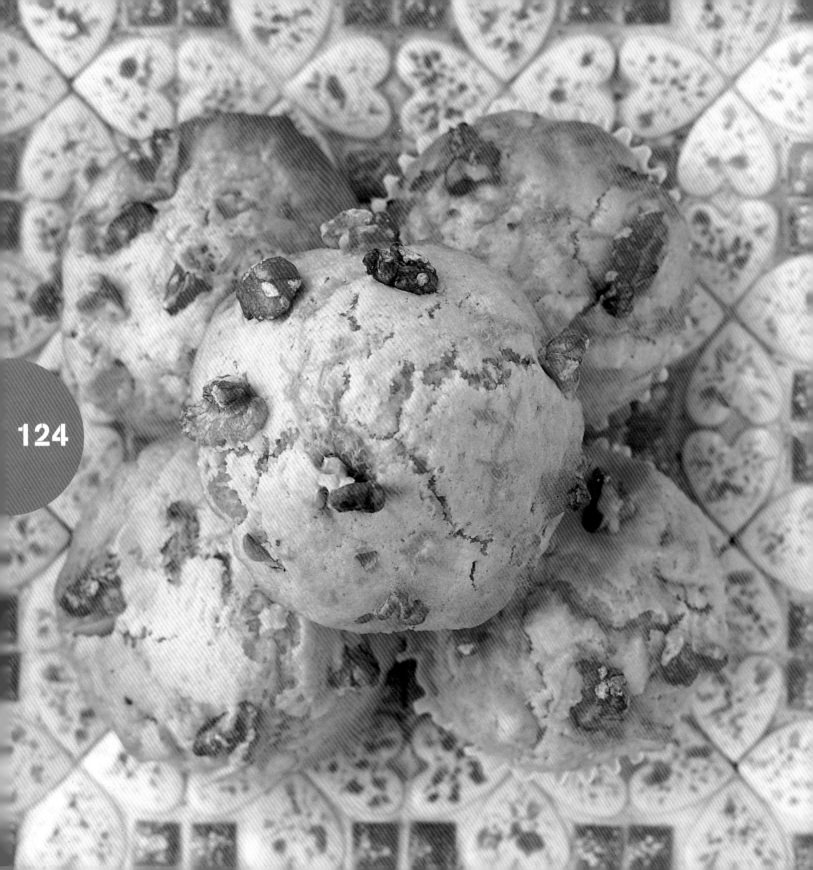

Carrot-Apple Muffins

Mid-morning or mid-afternoon snack! Move over Nigella, Jamie and Martha, you too can be a baking genius with this recipe ... Makes: 12 muffins

Tools:

measure cups/spoons
knife & cutting board
mixing bowls
1 large muffin pan
paper liners or parchment paper

Shopping list:

* olive oil spray
* 2 cups (10 oz) plain (all-purpose) flour
* 2 teaspoons baking soda
* 1 teaspoon cinnamon
* $1/2$ teaspoon ground ginger powder
* $1/2$ teaspoon ground cardamom (optional)
* $1/4$ teaspoon salt
* $1 1/4$ cups (10 oz) sugar
* 1 large carrot
* 2 green apples
* 3 large eggs
* 1 teaspoon vanilla extract
* 1 teaspoon freshly squeezed orange juice
* $1/2$ cup (4 fl oz) vegetable oil
* $1/2$ cup (4 oz) yogurt or buttermilk
* $1/4$ cup (1 oz) chopped walnuts

How to make it:

1 Preheat oven to 180°C (350°F). Spray the muffin cups or paper (if using).

2 In a bowl, sift together all the dry ingredients and spices. Grate the carrots and apples, reserving some for garnishing the top of the muffins. Toss through the dry flour mix.

3 In another bowl, mix together the wet ingredients, and then incorporate the dry into the wet. Don't over-mix as it needs to be lumpy.

4 Spoon mixture into the muffin pan. Top with the reserved carrot and apple mix and sprinkle over walnuts.

5 Bake in the center of the oven for 15-20 minutes until golden and puffed up, and when a skewer inserted into the center comes out clean; remove.

6 Allow muffins to cool in the pan on a baking rack for 5 minutes before turning out on a serving platter. They look great dusted with icing (confectioner's) sugar too! They will keep in an airtight container at room temperature for 5 days, or can be frozen for one month (defrost and warm them in the oven).

125

Substitute pear for the apples and zucchinis for carrots.

Avocado Bruschetta

We were inspired to create this version of bruschetta from our favorite beach café. Great after a morning swim or yoga or just as a pick-me-up at the early end of a long working day ... Serves: 2 or more people, depending on how hungry you are (or rather, how many laps you swam!)

Tools:

grill pan or toaster
small pastry-style brush
knife & cutting board
mixing bowl & wooden spoon

Shopping list:

* 4 slices Turkish bread, cut long & about 2 cm ($^3/_4$ inch) thick
* 1 tablespoon olive oil
* 1 clove garlic, peeled & smashed sea salt flakes and ground pepper
* 1 avocado
* 2 yellow tomatoes
* $^1/_2$ teaspoon red chili paste
* 1 lime, squeezed
* 2 sprigs coriander (cilantro) leaves

How to make it:

1 Heat the grill pan (if using) on high until almost smoking. Brush the bread with the olive oil, and place in the grill pan or pop in the toaster. Keep an eye on it either way, making sure the bread charrs slightly but doesn't burn. Turn over to do the second side if using the pan.

2 When done, rub the garlic clove over one side of the bread and season with salt and pepper. Keep warm.

3 Peel and slice the avocado and slice the tomato quite finely.

4 Mix the chili paste and lime juice together in a small bowl to make a little vinaigrette.

5 Arrange the tomato, then the avocado on the bread. Tear the coriander leaves slightly. Spoon the chili dressing over the bruschetta, season with salt and pepper and top with a sprinkle of the coriander.

HOT TIP

You can **melt a little bit of cheese** onto the bread or even grate soy cheese if you don't do dairy. Then top with either just the avocado or the tomato or both. Don't pile it up too high or it will fall off before it gets to your mouth (but your pet will love you for it!).

126

Any bread works — perhaps try pita or just plain toasted wholemeal (wholewheat) bread or even English muffins.

HOT TIPS:

The process of fast boiling and then plunging green vegetables into cold water stops all the vitamins leeching into the water. Remember to never cover them when cooking, as this turns them brown – and they're next to useless to you in a nutritional sense then!

Substitute any ingredients to your heart's content. Anything goes with this salad! Just remember to cook the vegetables that you like separately and assemble it at the end.

128

Drew's Salad

We call this the "kitchen sink" salad – you can put anything from your fridge in this so pull on your master chef's hat and feel free to improvize a little. Serves: 2 people - more if you beef up the ingredients

Tools

knife & cutting board
2 small saucepans & strainer
mixing bowls & wooden spoon
jar with lid to make the dressing

Shopping list:

For the salad:
* 4 medium-sized new potatoes
* 1 teaspoon salt
* 1 bunch snake beans
* 1 bunch broccoli rabe
* 1 small carrot
* 2 organic brown eggs
* 1 small bag snow pea sprouts
* $1/4$ cup ($1^1/_2$ oz) almonds

For the honey Dijon dressing:
* olive oil
* 2 tablespoons honey
* 1 tablespoon Dijon mustard
* white wine vinegar
* $1/2$ garlic clove, minced
* salt & pepper

How to make it:

1 Lightly scrub the potatoes and quarter them. Place in a small saucepan and cover with water, adding salt. Bring gently to a boil and cook until "fork tender" - this means until a fork slides gently into the potato but with some resistance.

2 Trim and clean the green vegetables. Meanwhile, bring a small saucepan of water to a boil.

3 "Blanch" the snake beans and broccoli rabe. This means cooking them lightly in boiling salted water, then immediately plunging them into a strainer over a bowl filled with ice cubes and water to stop the cooking process and keep them green. When cool enough to handle, cut the beans down into 6 cm ($2^1/_2$ inch) lengths and do the same for the broccoli rabe.

4 Fill hal f a small saucepan with water, add a dash of white vinegar and salt to it and bring to a boil. When boiling rapidly, turn to a medium heat and gently place the eggs in the water. Use a timer to cook the eggs for 6 minutes. If you cook them too hard (i.e. the water is boiling rapidly) you will see a slight ring around the yolk after peeling. When done, plunge them into cold water so they are easier to peel. Peel and cut into halves.

5 Peel carrot and cut into matchstick-sized pieces.

6 Assemble all dressing ingredients into the jar, tighten the lid and shake to combine.

7 Place all the vegetables into your serving bowl. Pour over some of the dressing and toss lightly with a spoon. Add more dressing to taste and garnish with the snow pea sprouts.

With salad dressings the basic rule of thumb is three parts (spoons) oil to one part vinegar.

12-3PM

129

This salad keeps for 2 days in the fridge and tastes even better on the second day.

Japanese Nori Salad

A fresh vegetable salad that can be a side dish for other Japanese dishes or a main. Serves: 2 large portions or 4 side portions

Shopping list:

For the salad base:
* 1 large English (hothouse) or continental (telegraph) cucumber, washed & dried
* 1 large fresh carrot, washed and peeled
* 2 stalks of rainbow beet or celery, washed & dried
* 50 g (1¾ oz) snow peas, washed & dried
* 1 packet nori (as much of this or as little as you like)

For the dressing:
* 2 tablespoons sesame oil
* 2 tablespoons mirin
* 1 tablespoon brown rice vinegar
* sea salt flakes, to taste
* 2 dashes chili oil

How to make it:

1 Cut the cucumber into thirds, then slice it into thin strips lengthwise. Repeat for the carrot, making sure the cut side is laid down on the cutting board. This makes it stable while doing more slicing. (Be sure to take care with the sharp knife.)

2 Slice the rainbow beet or the celery on long "bias" (angled cuts) against the grain. Make a fine shred of the snow peas on the bias as well. Toss vegetables together in a large bowl and cover.

3 To make the dressing, find a jar with a tight-fitting lid. Pour all ingredients into it and shake well until combined. Keep cool until you are going to serve the salad.

4 Using scissors, cut the nori sheet into matchstick-sized pieces and keep in a plastic bag until you are ready to serve.

To Serve: Shake jar once again to recombine the ingredients and pour over the salad. Toss the nori strips (hold a few back) into the salad and carefully combine all, using tongs or salad forks to make sure the dressing coats all the vegetables. Garnish with the remaining nori shreds.

note
The best thing about this dish is that you can put just about **any vegetable** in it, and you can make it as simple or as complex as you like.

It can be a lunch in itself — take it to work in a tupperware container — or it can be a pre-dinner appetiser.

we used
rainbow
beet for its
folic acid &
vitamin K

BE CREATIVE: IT'S A SALAD

try this!

Try substituting canned salmon
for tuna if you want variety.
Leftover roast tomatoes can go
in – in fact any leftover roast
vegies would go perfectly in this
salad. Check the fridge!

Any greens can be added in,
e.g. rocket (arugula), shredded
spinach and baby field greens.

Picnic Pasta Salad

Pack this up the night before for a picnic day or car trip. This salad has no real quantities as it is really up to your taste and imagination! Serves: 4 people

Tools
knife & cutting board
saucepan & strainer
mixing bowl & wooden spoon
Tupperware container

Shopping list:
* 250 g (8 oz) dry or packet pasta such as penne
* 2 x 100 g (3½ oz) cans tuna, in olive oil, flavored or plain
* 1 punnet (tub) fresh cherry tomatoes
* 1 bunch green onions
* 1 red onion, chopped
* fresh herbs such as chives, parsley & basil, picked to taste
* balsamic vinegar
* salt & pepper

How to make it:

1 Cook pasta according to the packet directions. Drain and keep warm.

2 Drain tuna into a bowl to collect the flavored olive oil it's packed in. Toss oil over the warm pasta. Flake the tuna with a fork and toss through the pasta.

3 Cut the cherry tomatoes in half. Slice the green and red onions and add to the salad. Tear or cut the herbs with scissors.

4 Toss gently into pasta and tuna, then drizzle balsamic vinegar over the top and season with pepper and salt.

5 Put in your best picnic container – be it good old Tupperware, a beautiful ceramic plate with a kitchen cloth to cover or even Chinese take-away boxes!

Save some herbs for a final garnish on the top.
Best eaten straight from the container!

Couscous Salad

This salad keeps for about 3 days in the fridge and makes a fab lunch on its own, or eaten with some fish or other meat, if you prefer, as part of a more filling dinner.

Tools
knife & cutting board
medium & small saucepan
mixing bowl
small frying pan

Shopping list:
* 1 packet couscous (about 220 g/7 oz)
* 2 cups (16 fl oz) vegetable or chicken stock
* 1/2 cup (4 fl oz) olive oil
* 1 lemon, zested & juiced
* 2 tablespoons white wine vinegar
* salt & pepper
* 1/3 cup (1 1/4 oz) of each of the following dried fruits: apricots, cranberries, figs, mangoes
* 1 tablespoon chopped crystallized ginger
* 2 mini cucumbers or 1/2 standard-sized continental (telegraph) cucumber
* 200 g (6 1/2 oz) marinated feta cheese
* 1 small red onion
* 1/2 bunch dill
* 1/2 bunch mint
* 1/4 bunch Italian (flat leaf) parsley
* 1/2 cup (2 1/2 oz) sliced almonds

How to make it:

1 Cook the couscous with the stock according to the packet directions. Drain if necessary and keep warm.

2 Mix together the olive oil, lemon zest and juice, vinegar and salt & pepper. Place in small saucepan and heat gently until just warm.

3 While heating the dressing, roughly chop the dried fruit into similar sizes. Mix with the crystallized ginger in the serving bowl and pour the warmed dressing over.

4 Dice up the cucumber, feta, onion and toss into the serving bowl, mixing with the dried fruits and coating with the dressing.

5 Scoop the couscous out of the saucepan and into the serving bowl, tossing gently with the spoon to mix all the ingredients and dressing.

6 Tear the fresh herbs - leave some large pieces as they're part of the look and taste - and add to the salad.

7 Heat a small frying pan and when hot, add the almonds and keep the pan moving to toast the nuts but not burn them. When golden, mix half into the salad and reserve the other half as a garnish.

It often tastes better if it's prepared ahead of time so the flavors come out. You can make this salad the night before you need it.

135

Hot tips!

The amount of stock you use could vary slightly depending on the packet instructions. The best guide is to go with the texture, it shouldn't make the mix too runny. You could add water to reach 2 cups (16 fl oz).

Most grains would work with this - quinoa, rice, amaranth etc. Investigate the bins at the wholefoods market! **Any other dried fruits** such as plums or pineapple will also be tasty. Orange juice can take the place of the lemon juice and most vinegars (except balsamic) will be tasty!

136

Hot tip: *Just so you know, only in Australia do they serve bacon in this salad! It was not part of the original recipe developed by the waiter himself, so don't worry if you don't eat pork or if you don't have any to hand!*

Easy Caesar Salad

A few "pre-fab" ingredients, plus the freshest lettuce and cheese and some freshly baked Turkish bread and you have a speedy snack or lunch. Try topping with a simple grilled chicken, prawns (shrimp) or just go vego-style. Serves: 1 person

Tools:
knife & cutting board
baking dish (sheet)
salad spinner
mixing bowl & tongs
grater or peeler

Shopping list:

For the dressing:
* 2 tablespoons low-fat mayonnaise; it can even be a soy-based one
* 2 teaspoons lemon juice
* 1 teaspoon white wine vinegar
* $\frac{1}{2}$ teaspoon Worcestershire sauce
* $\frac{1}{4}$ teaspoon Tabasco
* $\frac{1}{4}$ teaspoon garlic puree (optional)
* 1 tablespoon grated Parmesan cheese
* salt & pepper

For the salad:
* 2 slices Turkish bread
* $\frac{1}{2}$ tablespoon olive oil
* 1 clove garlic, peeled
* salt & pepper
* 1 baby cos (Romaine) lettuce head
* 30 g (1 oz) Parmesan cheese, shaved

How to make the dressing:

1 Mix together all the dressing ingredients in a small bowl until it is creamy and to taste. Add as much or as little of these ingredients as you feel comfortable with.

How to make the salad:

2 Cut the bread into cubes, and heat a small frying pan.

3 Put olive oil and garlic (if using) in the pan. When garlic starts to sizzle, add the bread cubes and salt & pepper then stir to coat with the oil. Keep heat on low so the croutons go golden and crispy without burning.

4 Wash the lettuce and spin dry. Tear into bite-sized pieces into your serving bowl.

5 Add the croutons to the bowl and the dressing and, using the tongs, toss to coat everything evenly.

6 Shave or grate or crumble the Parmesan cheese over the top. Add some salt and pepper over the top. At this point you can add grilled vegetables, chicken or fish as you prefer.

Vegie Salad Sandwich

We know everyone can make a sandwich, but can you make a healthy one? In our version, you can substitute any items but be sure to keep it light and healthy. A salad sandwich is a great fail-safe way to get tonnes of vitamins and minerals into your system. Banish commercially made and sugar-loaded white bread and bring on the yeast-free, wholemeal (wholewheat) and spelt bread versions.

Tools:
knife & cutting board

Shopping list:
- 3 slices low-carb soy bread or any multigrain wheat bread
- 3 tablespoons hummus
- 1 cup (1 oz) baby spinach leaves or rocket (arugula) leaves
- 1 punnet (tub) sprouts - snow peas, alfafa or micro greens
- 1 fresh tomato (any type)
- 1 continental (telegraph) cucumber
- 1 avocado, sliced & with a little lemon juice squeezed over or splashed with vinegar
- 250 g (8 oz) goat's cheese or low-fat cream cheese or soy cheese spread
- 1 jar tomato chutney or tomato jam
- salt & pepper

How to make it:

1 Lay out the three slices of bread and spread one tablespoon of hummus on each slice.

2 Use one slice as the bottom of the sandwich. Start by layering the spinach leaves, sprouts, tomato and cucumber, then top with the avocado and preferred cheese. Season with salt & pepper and finish with a dollop of the tomato chutney. Cover with the second piece of bread, hummus side up. Repeat the process.

3 Cover with the third piece of bread. Press down firmly with the palm of your hand, to meld all the components and to make it easier to cut in half.

4 You don't have to eat this all at once - perhaps wrap up the two halves and use the second half as your mid-afternoon snack: it is quite filling!

try this!

You can use **Skye's pesto sauce** [p 164] as a subsitute for the hummus.

Garnish with
a little
sesame seeds,
almonds &
coriander
(cilantro).

This salad will become second nature once you practice a
little. Remember, the secret's in the marinade!

Chinese Chicken Salad

A simple classic – and another good staple in every girlo's cooking repertoire. If you can get hold of some of the take-away cartons from your local Chinese, they make a fun presentation and a handy picnic pack. You can halve the recipe if you want to make it for one person – it'll be 2 days' worth though! Serves: 6 people

Shopping list:

For the marinade:
- 1 cup (8 fl oz) soy sauce
- 2 tablsepoons five spice
- $\frac{1}{3}$ cup (3 fl oz) sesame oil

For the meat:
- 3 x 180 g (6 oz) chicken breast, trimmed & cleaned of white fat
- $\frac{1}{4}$ cup (2 fl oz) peanut oil

For the salad:
- 1 supermarket bag of mixed Asian greens (standard-sized pack)
- $\frac{1}{4}$ head of Chinese (napa) cabbage, finely "chiffonaded" (shredded) or sliced
- $\frac{1}{4}$ head of iceberg lettuce, chiffonaded
- 100 g ($3\frac{1}{2}$ oz) bean sprouts
- 6 green onions, sliced on the bias
- 2 carrots, peeled & grated
- dim sum (potsticker) wrappers cut into fine matchstick slices
- 120 g (4 oz) sliced almonds, toasted
- 30 g (1 oz) or 2 tablespoons toasted sesame seeds
- 12 coriander (cilantro) sprigs

For the dressing:
- $\frac{1}{3}$ cup (3 fl oz) soy sauce
- $\frac{1}{3}$ cup (3 fl oz) sesame or peanut oil
- $\frac{1}{3}$ cup (3 fl oz) rice vinegar
- 2 tablespoons mirin

How to make it:

1 Mix the marinade ingredients together, pour over the chicken breasts and allow to marinate in the fridge for 2 hours. Strain liquid, reserve in a jug (pitcher).

2 Mix soy sauce, sesame oil and mirin together in a jar with a tight-fitting lid. Shake to combine, add seasonings to taste.

3 Preheat oven to 180°C (350°F). Heat half the peanut oil in a non-stick frying pan and sear chicken breasts on each side for about one minute, placing in a foil or baking dish (sheet) when done.

4 Pour over reserved marinade, and cook in oven for a further 15 minutes. Discard marinade. Cool and slice chicken on the bias into bite-sized pieces.

5 Wipe out pan, heat rest of peanut oil and fry dim sum wrappers until crispy. Drain on paper towels.

6 Assemble the salad greens and vegetables in one large bowl. Pour over some salad dressing, divide salad among your bowls or containers.

7 Add chicken to each bowl and pour over some more dressing. Garnish with more coriander sprigs, sesame seeds, dim sum strips and almonds. Serve immediately.

Salmon Avocado Maki Rolls

Japanese food is extremely healthy. With its emphasis on seaweed and soy, plus raw fish in many of the key dishes, it is something girlo chefs will gain a lot from. It takes a bit of practice, but don't be deterred, it's quite easy once you get the hang of it! To make these delicious and nutritious snacks, you need to do one prep-ahead step. Serves: 4 people

SUSHI RICE USING A RICE COOKER. Cook the rice according to the maker's manual including changing the volume of water needed. Then go to sushi rice step 3.

Tools:

measuring cup
mesh colander
saucepan & lid
1 sushi rolling mat
plastic wrap
small bowl of warm water
with teaspoon vinegar for
cleaning fingers

Shopping list:

For the sushi rice:
- 1 cup (7 oz) short-grain rice
- 1½ cups (12 fl oz) water
- 3 tablespoons brown rice vinegar
- 1 tablespoon honey

For the maki rolls:
- 1 packet nori sheets
- 2 tablespoons wasabi paste, or keep handy and add to taste
- 100 g (3½ oz) smoked salmon
- 100 g (3½ oz) pickled ginger or to taste
- 1 avocado, sliced thinly lengthwise
- salt & pepper
- light salt soy sauce, to serve

How to make sushi rice:

1 Wash rice three times in a mesh colander until water runs clear.

2 Place washed rice and water in small saucepan with a tight-fitting lid. Bring to a boil, then turn down heat to a low simmer and place lid on for about 12 minutes. Turn off heat and let sit for 5 more minutes to steam before removing lid.

3 Meanwhile, heat up rice vinegar and honey in a small pan on low heat until melted together. Pour mix over steamed rice and gently mix through with a wooden spoon. Taste to make sure it has a sweet-tart flavor. Placing a cloth over top to keep warm.

How to make the rolls:

1 Lay out the mat and cover with plastic wrap to stop rice falling between cracks!

2 Lay a piece of nori on the mat, shiny side down.

3 Cover ¾ of the nori with the sushi rice – use the back of a wooden spoon to smooth it down to the edges. Use the small bowl of vinegar water to cleanse your fingers of all that sticky rice!

4 Smear a teaspoon of wasabi paste along the shorter bottom edge closest to you. Beware, it can be really hot! Taste a bit first to check and proceed with care.

5 Lay ¼ of the salmon slightly overlapping pieces across half the rice.

6 Scatter some pickled ginger over the salmon to the edges of the rice.

7 Lay the sliced avocado on top, season with the salt & pepper.

8 Gathering both corners of short end of mat, start rolling mat up and

Top tip If you don't want to overdo the wasabi leave it out and just serve with the soy sauce in a dish on the side instead.

143

away from you. Keep top of roll tucked under to ensure it holds and hold firmly with your fingers. Sometimes it's easier to hold end with one hand and roll with the other. Once you have a cylinder, run your fingers along left to right side to smooth out the roll. Release from the mat and keep chilled. Repeat with the remaining ingredients.

9 Place the first roll onto a cutting board. Cut the roll in half. Cut each half in half again, on an angle, so you get a wedge shape. Arrange on your platter with the wedge back in the center; smear some wasabi paste in one corner and the rest of the pickled ginger in the other. Serve soy sauce on the side or drizzle it over the top.

MISO SOUP

There are so many ways to make miso soup and on top of that there are quite a few varieties of miso paste. It can be red, brown or yellow or even white. Method, aging and taste account for these – experiment to find the one you like. To make this recipe, we used organic miso soup powder packets, as we can travel with these and have them on hand at a moment's notice. Serves: 2 people

Shopping list:
* 4 cups (32 fl oz) water
* 100 g (3½ oz) tofu (silky, firm or smoked)
* 50 g (1¾ oz) button mushrooms
* 2 stalks green onion
* 2 packets miso mix or 4 tablespoons fresh miso

How to make it:

1 Boil the water in a small saucepan. While that is boiling, prepare the tofu plus other vegetables. Cut the tofu into tiny fingernail-sized cubes. Slice the mushrooms and the green onions and keep together in a small bowl on the counter.

2 Add the miso paste or mix to the boiling water and stir to combine.

3 Turn the water down to simmer and add the tofu and the remaining ingredients. Save some onions for garnish as they do sink to the bottom of the bowl.

4 Taste. If you want it stronger, add more of the miso packet mix or paste.

5 Serve in bowls with Asian spoons on the side and use the reserved vegetables for the garnish just before you serve!

Shiitake mushrooms, shredded spinach or nori can be added to bulk it up.

spy-skinned Fish Tacos

With red cabba[ge], garlic crema, and pico de gallo. A healthier versi[on of] the fast food option so it's Mexican tonight at you[r] acienda! Serves: 2 people

Tools
knife & cutting board
mixing bowl & wooden spoon
juicer
measure cups/spoons
grilling pan (broiler) or use barbecue

Shopping list:

For the cabbage slaw:
* 1/4 red cabbge
* 1/2 red onion
* 1/4 fresh pineapple
* salt & pepper
* squeeze of lime juice, to taste

For the garlic crema (cream):
* 1/2 cup (4 fl oz) crème fraiche or sour cream
* 1 clove garlic, crushed
* 1 tablespoon lime juice

For the coriander pesto:
* 1 bunch coriander (cilantro) leaves
* 1 garlic clove, crushed
* 1/4 cup (2 fl oz) olive oil
* 2 limos, zested & juiced
* 1 tablespoon pepita seeds
* salt & pepper
* 1 tablespoon water

For the pico de gallo:
* 4 tomatoes
* 1 red onion
* 1/2 fresh thai chili
* 1/4 bunch fresh coriander (cilantro)
* juice of 1 lime
* salt & pepper
* chili oil

For the tacos:
* 1 teaspoon cumin
* 1/2 teaspoon chili powder
* sea salt & pepper
* 1 garlic clove, minced
* juice of 1 lime
* 1 tablespoon olive oil
* 4 sprigs coriander (cilantro), for garnish
* 4 crispy taco shells
* 180 g (6 oz) salmon fillet, skin on

How to make it:

1 Cabbage slaw: Finely slice cabbage and red onion, toss together with sliced fresh pineapple and season with salt, pepper and a squeeze of lime juice.

2 Garlic cream: Mix all ingredients together and place in fridge to sit and blend flavors.

3 Coriander pesto: Mix all ingredients in a blender until pureed and bright green. Place in a bowl covered with foil until needed.

4 Pico de g[allo]: chop all and toss toge[ther in a] container with a tight-fitting lid. Allow to marinate in fridge until needed. Check seasonings before serving and adjust where needed. It can be spicier, more piquant, saltier, to your tastes.

5 Crispy skinned fish: Mix all ingredients except the fish. Pour mixture over the fillet and let stand for 1 hour in the fridge.

6 Place a grilling pan on stove, or use a barbecue, and preheat to 180°C (350°F).

7 Wipe oil over pan or grill then sear fillet skin side down first for 3 minutes. Flip on the flesh side and cook for 3 minutes. Flip back onto the skin for a final 2 minutes to crisp up skin. Remove to a plate.

8 Slice the fillet into 4 fingers.

9 Fill each taco shell with the cabbage slaw, then add the fish and top with the pico de gallo, garlic crema and finish with coriander pesto.

This is also fab served with a side of guacamole! [page 153]

We used salmon fillets for this dish – but the best ones are fish like swordfish, barramundi and coral trout, all of which work well with the flavors. Prawns (shrimp) would also be yummy, as would calamari. You can go wild with this one!

For serving up a real feast, use trays and colorful paper napkins and mexican votive candles for a bright night in Frida-Kahlo style …

147

Serve with pita bread that has been brushed
with olive oil and lightly toasted

148

A great
snack while
you're out
and about!

Hot tip

You can substitute
the chickpeas for any
kind of bean to make
a "hummus" e.g., red
kidney beans, black
beans or navy beans.
Experiment a little by
changing the flavors &
seasonings.

Spiced Chickpeas & Easy Hummus

A wonderful source of protein for vegetarians, these versatile little legumes are easiest from the can – packed in plain water and organic if possible. Chickpeas make a great afternoon pick-me-up snack that gives lasting energy – great if you have to gear up for a night out on the town. Hold the fries! Serves: a cocktail party or 2 hungry people

Tools:

small frying pan
knife & cutting board
mixing bowls, wooden spoons
grater & juicer
You will need a food processor to make hummus!

Shopping list:

For spiced chickpeas:
* 1 teaspoon each: paprika, cumin, chili powder, turmeric, sea salt
* 1 tablespoon olive oil
* 400 g (13 oz) can cooked chickpeas, strained & rinsed
* 1 lemon, zested & juiced

For hummus:
* 400 g (13 oz) can chickpeas, strained & rinsed
* 2 garlic cloves, peeled & smashed
* 1 lemon, zested & juiced
* 1 teaspoon each cumin, cayenne, salt & pepper
* 1 tablespoon extra virgin olive oil
* 1 tablespoon sesame oil
* $\frac{1}{4}$ cup (2 fl oz) chicken or vegetable stock
* 1 packet pita bread

How to make spiced chickpeas:

1 Heat small frying pan on low while you mix the spices.

2 Add olive oil to the pan then add spices, stirring gently to make sure they toast lightly and become fragrant.

3 Add chickpeas and toss in the pan to coat with the spices. Pour in lemon juice and turn up the heat to evaporate the liquids.

4 When they look golden and even a little charred in places, turn the heat off and tip onto a dinner plate with absorbent paper to soak up excess oils. Season to taste. Can be served hot or cold.

How to make the hummus:

1 Place chickpeas, garlic, zest and seasonings in the bowl of the food processor and start to churn. Through the funnel, pour in the oils, the lemon juice and blend until creamy. Use the vegetable or chicken stock to create the dip-like consistency – you may need more than $\frac{1}{4}$ cup, you may need less. This is better for you than using too much stock, which, apart from adding unnecessary fat, makes it a bit rich for some people's taste.

2 Adjust and taste the seasonings according to how you like it! Serve with spiced chickpeas and pita bread. Hummus is a great sandwich spread, dip or appetizer. It keeps for 4 days in the fridge when covered.

Grilled Vegetable Quesadillas

We find loads of inspiration in Tex Mex cooking. This is a healthy and quick snack for girlo chefs who just love to go south of the border. Ariba! Makes: 4 quesadillas - 4 people for lunch or 8 people as an appetizer snack

Tools:
knife & cutting board
mixing bowl
non-stick frying pan
pastry brush

Shopping list:
* olive oil
* 1 small eggplant or $1/4$ of a large eggplant
* 1 yellow squash, sliced
* 1 green zucchini
* 1 rib silverbeet (Swiss chard) or celery
* $1/2$ red onion, sliced
* 1 red capiscum (bell pepper)
* 1 yellow capsicum (bell pepper)
* $1/2$ teaspoon chili flakes
* 1 teaspoon cumin
* salt & pepper
* 1 bunch fresh coriander (cilantro) sprigs, chopped
* 330 g (11 oz) goat's cheese log
* 250 g (8 oz) shredded Monterey Jack, cheddar or mozzarella cheese
* 4 flour tortilla shells - plain, tomato or corn flavored

How to make it:

1 Heat a non-stick pan on medium heat and lightly brush with olive oil.

2 Cut all vegetables in half lengthwise and then again if very thick (e.g. eggplant).

3 Lay vegetables on the board and slice against each length to get a half moon or matchstick shape. They should be similar in thickness for cooking purposes.

4 Toss with the olive oil, chili flakes, cumin, salt & pepper and coriander sprigs in a bowl.

5 Toss in the frying pan in batches to sear and soften. Place in a medium-sized mixing bowl. Crumble goat's cheese over when cool.

6 Scoop out about a $1/2$ cup of mixture per tortilla shell, and place on one half of the shell. Mix with $1/4$ of the shredded cheese, fold in half and brush with olive oil.

7 Place "half moon" shape in a hot frying pan and cook until it slightly blackens and crispens up. Turn over and cook until cheese is melted and center is hot.

8 Place on a plate or platter at the back of the stove, covered loosely with foil to keep warm while you repeat the process until all the mix is gone. Serve warm.

Hot tip: You may find that the vegetables yield more than 4 shells can hold, in which case, just freeze the raw quesadilla mix for a quick snack another day.

150

Make it atmospheric place votive candles in brown paper bags with 7.5 cm (3 inches) of sand or soil in the bottom. Roll down the top of the paper bags and open wide. Light the candle and place safely in the garden for a classic ambience. Wear a poncho or sombrero and you'll be ready to party Mexican-style!

151

152

Hot Tip:
To make sure the
avocado is ripe,
hold it in the palm
of your hand and
squeeze very
gently. It should
feel firm, but
give a fraction of
a second later.
Also, the brown
stem tip will fall
off if prodded.

Zesty Guacamole

Avocado, chilies and limes are a match made in food heaven. We can't fully claim this recipe as ours - the Aztecs have been eating this for thousands of years - but it's one we would absolutely have to have if we were ever stranded on a tropical island! Serves: For us, this is 1 serving, but to be a bit restrained - and perhaps healthier! - this is for about 4 people!

Tools

knife & cutting board
mixing bowl & wooden spoon
juicer
baking dish (sheet)

Shopping list:

* 2 avocadoes
* 2 limes, juiced
* sea salt & pepper
* 1 teaspoon chili paste
* 4 green onions, finely sliced
* 4 flour tortillas
* non-stick oil spray
* 1 bag tortilla chips - we prefer organic ones!

How to make it:

1 Cut avocadoes in half around the equator. Using a large spoon, slip them out of their skins. Chop them roughly and place in the mixing bowl. Save the avocado pits.

2 Pour the lime juice over avocado, add the salt, pepper, chili paste and green onions. Mash with a wooden spoon, but leave it somewhat chunky.

3 Place in a ceramic, glass or wooden bowl with the avocado pits on the top to stop it going brown. Cover tightly with plastic wrap pressed into the mix and with another layer over the top.

4 Just before serving, layer fresh tortillas on a baking dish (sheet) that has been prepared with the non-stick oil spray. Bake for 5 minutes until softened and somewhat charred. Tear tortillas into pieces onto the serving platter with the tortilla chips. Make a space for the guacamole bowl, removing pits and plastic.

To store any leftovers, squeeze lime juice over the top and seal in a container.

Curry Sides: Coconut Raita, Mint Raita, Tomato Pickle

These are the "cooling" condiments used to tame the spice and heat of curries; they are also great afternoon snacks on their own. Serves: 4

Tools:
knife & cutting board
mixing bowls
grater, strainer, whisk & wooden spoon

Shopping list:

For coconut raita:
* 1 cup (4 oz) desiccated (unsweetened shredded) coconut
* ½ banana
* ½ cup (4 oz) plain non-fat yogurt, soy or dairy
* 1 tablespoon light coconut milk
* dash of vegetable oil
* salt & pepper

For mint raita:
* ½ continental (telegraph) cucumber, peeled
* ¼ bunch mint
* ½ cup (4 oz) yogurt
* 1 teaspoon garam masala (available in the supermarket)
* 1 tablespoon mint sauce

For tomato pickle:
* 1 large or 2 small tomatoes (any variety is good)
* 1 red onion
* ¼ bunch coriander (cilantro)
* 1 tablespoon white vinegar
* lime juice, salt & pepper, to taste

How to make cocunut raita:
1. Place coconut on a non-stick cookie pan and place in oven for 10 minutes or until lightly golden and crunchy.

2. Mix all the other ingredients except seasonings in a bowl with a wooden spoon until the banana is mashed.

3. Add the coconut and season with salt & pepper to taste. Cover and keep in fridge until needed.

How to make mint raita:
1. Grate the cucumber on the large holes of the grater into a strainer over a mixing bowl. Press down on the flesh to squeeze out as much of the cucumber liquid as possible. (This is great added to the filtered water you keep in your fridge!)

2. Finely shred the mint with a knife, and mix into the yogurt, then season with the garam masala. Add the mint sauce, taste for seasonings and add salt or more mint sauce for more tang. Combine with cucumber. Cover and keep in the fridge. Will keep for 3 days.

How to make tomato pickle:
1. Cut the tomato in half, scoop the flesh out and slice lengthwise. Cut the onion in half and slice about the same size as the tomato. Combine the two and add vinegar to the mix.

2. Tear the coriander and season to taste with the lime juice and salt. Let sit for 1 hour before using.

Serve them with pappadums or Turkish bread. Like the hummus recipe, these make great individual appetizers, to eat before dinner.

155

Hot Tips

The coconut raita will last for 3 days in the fridge even with the banana. If you omit the banana (which will still be tasty) it will last an additional 2 days.

These are great for the neighborhood fundraiser or for impressing visiting grannies. No one can resist cupcakes!

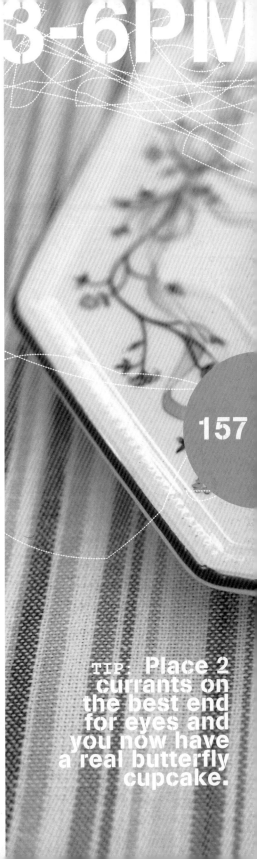

Butterfly Cupcakes

A lovely, girly treat for afternoon tea parties! Makes: about 12 large or 24 mini cupcakes

Tools:

paper liners for muffins
1 large muffin pan (12 cups)
measure cups/spoons
mixing bowls
knife & cutting board

Shopping list:

* non-stick oil spray
* 1 cup plain (all-purpose) flour
* 1 teaspoon baking powder
* pinch of salt
* $1/3$ cup (3 fl oz) whole or soy milk
* $1/2$ teaspoon vanilla essence
* 6 tablespoons unsalted butter, softened
* $3/4$ cup ($5^1/4$ oz) castor (superfine) sugar
* 1 large egg
* 1 small carton cream, loosely whipped
* 1 jar preferred jam - blackberry, strawberry or even rose petal
* icing (confectioner's) sugar

How to make it:

1 Preheat oven to 180°C (350°F). Spray paper liners and insert into muffin pan cups.

2 In a mixing bowl, combine flour, baking powder and salt. In another bowl stir together the milk and vanilla.

3 "Cream" the butter and sugar in a large bowl either by hand or with an electric mixer, until it is a pale lemony yellow color and creamy in texture. This will take about 4 minutes. Add egg and beat until just incorporated. Then add flour mix and the wet milk mix in alternating batches. Don't over-mix!

4 Spoon the batter into the muffin cups about two-thirds full. Bake until the tops are golden and puffy, about 15 minutes. Remove from oven, and wait for 5 minutes before inverting onto serving plate.

5 Once cooked, slice the puff top off the cake, and slice the top bit in half again.

6 Spoon the cream then the jam in a line down the center of the base, invert the cut top halves so that the cut side is exposed and they look like wings. Dust with icing sugar and serve.

Style your tea party with pretty serviettes, placemats and old-style floral plates — mix and match!

157

TIP: **Place 2 currants on the best end for eyes and you now have a real butterfly cupcake.**

Classic Chocolate Chip Cookies

What would life be without chocolate? Thankfully we'll never know! It's great to be able to wheel out such things as a batch of hot chocolate chip cookies on demand, especially if the girls are around. Be warned, they are incredibly Moorish ... Makes: about 24 medium-sized cookies

Tools:
. measure cups/spoons
  mixing bowls
  non-stick cookie pan

Shopping list:
* non-stick oil spray
* 3 cups (15 oz) plain (all-purpose) flour
* 1 1/2 teaspoons baking soda
* pinch of salt
* 1 cup (8 oz) butter
* 1 1/2 cups (10 1/2 oz) brown sugar
* 1 cup (8 oz) granulated sugar
* 1 1/2 teaspoons vanilla essence
* 3 eggs
* 2 cups (12 oz) semi-sweet chocolate, milk chocolate or white chocolate chips

How to make it:

1 Preheat oven to 180°C (350°F). Spray the paper liners and insert into cookie pan cups. Mix together the flour, baking soda and salt.

2 "Cream" the butter and sugar together in a large bowl either by hand or with an electric mixer, until it is a pale lemony yellow color and creamy in texture. This will take about 4 minutes. Mix in vanilla essence. In a separate bowl, beat one egg lightly with a fork then add gradually to the butter mix and beat a few times until just mixed in. Repeat with remaining 2 eggs, then add the flour mix and whatever chocolate chips you are using. Don't over-mix! (See hot tip below.)

3 Lay a sheet of plastic wrap on the counter and scoop the mix into a log in the middle. Roll up the wrap like a sausage and smooth it out. Twist the ends to keep it airtight and place in the fridge for 30 minutes.

4 Using a medium- to small-sized ice cream scoop or a knife to cut off slices, roll the pieces into balls and flatten with the back of a spoon. Place on cookie pan.

5 Bake until golden, 9–11 minutes, for a soft American-style cookie or 12–15 minutes for a crispier one.

6 Any leftover dough can be frozen for up to 3 months.

HOT TIP: Be careful not to over-mix the butter as you may "curdle" it and this ruins it. Beat carefully – less is more!

For those girlo chefs who
have the willpower: you can
freeze the batter in small
portions, and only make
one at a time - if you
can bear it!

159

love it

Pumpkin Soup

Another favorite! The perfect heartwarmer for that evening in front of the TV! Pumpkin soup sustains us through many a cold day and night – we live on this, especially in winter. Serves: a number of cold, hungry people

Tools:
knife & cutting board
baking dish (sheet)
metal spoon
2 medium saucepans
6 cup Tupperware container
wooden spoon, ladle
blender

Shopping list:
* 1 pumpkin (butternut squash), about 1 kg (2 lb), peeled & seeded
* olive oil
* 4 sprigs fresh lemon thyme
* salt & pepper
* 1 red onion, chopped
* 1 knob ginger, peeled & grated
* 2 cloves garlic, crushed
* 2 tablespoons olive oil
* $1/2$ orange, zested & juiced
* 4 cups (32 fl oz) vegetable stock

How to make it:

1 Preheat oven to 200°C (400°F). Dice pumpkin into 3 cm (1$1/4$ inch) cubes; coat with olive oil, thyme, salt & pepper by tossing in a bowl. Place on the baking dish (sheet) and roast in the oven for about 30 minutes or until tender and slightly caramelized and golden. You will only need half the cubes – freeze the rest for future use after cooling (or use them for the risotto on page 160). Save a few cubes as a soup garnish.

2 Sautee together onion, ginger and garlic in olive oil until translucent and slightly sizzling. Add orange zest and juice.

3 Add the zest and the orange juice. Add the pumpkin cubes and the stock, and simmer gently for 30 minutes.

4 Cool slightly, then puree the pumpkin mix in batches in the blender, covering the top with a cloth to prevent splatters.

5 Pour the blended soup into the Tupperware container to store. To serve, reheat in a pot, adjust seasonings and serve into bowls.

Try these substitutes: Leeks for onion; chicken stock for vegetable stock; normal thyme or parsley for lemon thyme.

Hot tip!
By using more beans in the minestrone than pasta, it is a little bit healthier and good for vegetarians who need to ensure their protein intake is at the correct levels.

Quick Minestrone

Long winters without soup are lonely ones indeed. Don't be put off by what looks like the longest shopping list ever, this minestrone is a cracker! The ingredients can mostly be bought at a grocery store. Do a one-stop shop and in no time at all you'll have real soup for the soul. Serves: 4 people

Tools

knife & cutting board
medium-sized saucepan
measure cups & spoons

Shopping list:

* 1 tablespoon olive oil
* 1 white onion, diced
* 1 garlic clove, minced
* 1 teaspoon minced fresh thyme leaves
* 1 teaspoon minced fresh oregano
* 2 teaspoon minced fresh parsley
* $1/4$ teaspoon chili flakes
* 1 red capsicum (bell pepper), seeded & diced
* 1 yellow capsicum (bell pepper), seeded & diced
* 1 small eggplant, diced
* 1 carrot, peeled & diced
* 2 stalks celery
* 1 medium zucchini, diced
* 1 L (32 fl oz) V8 juice
* 400 g (13 oz) can white beans, drained & rinsed
* 400 g (13 oz) can cannellini beans, drained & rinsed
* 400 g (13 oz) can small kidney beans, drained & rinsed
* $1/4$ cup ($1^3/4$ oz) small pasta such as shells
* salt & pepper, to tate
* 1 cup (8 fl oz) warm water, as required

How to make it:

1 Put the olive oil, onion, garlic, herbs and spices in a saucepan and sautee until sizzling and you can smell the garlic. Add the vegetables and stir until they soften.

2 Pour in the V8 juice and stir. Add the beans.

3 When the vegetables feel almost cooked, add the pasta.

4 Taste and add salt & pepper. If the liquid is looking low, add some warm water. Serve in deep bowls with sides of bruschetta or bread rolls.

If you don't need to serve four people this keeps in the fridge for a few days and it freezes really well.

163

Cut everything the same size as the pasta you use so that it cooks evenly.

Skye's Pesto Pasta

This is an adaptation of my friend Skye's classic recipe, which she brought back from a trip to Italy. I have been fortunate to eat this many times at her home and I have never tasted a better pesto anywhere. Pesto sauce can be used in so many ways, not just over pasta. You'll never go hungry if there's pesto in the fridge! Serves: 4 people

Tools:
food processor or blender
Tupperware container
medium saucepan
strainer
knife & cutting board
wooden spoon

Shopping list:
For pesto:
* 2 cloves garlic
* 50 g (1³/₄ oz) toasted pine nuts
* 100 g (3¹/₂ oz) grated Parmesan
* 1 cup (8 fl oz) olive oil
* ¹/₄ bunch mint
* ¹/₄ bunch Italian (flat leaf) parsley
* 2 pinches fresh coriander (cilantro)
* 2 bunches basil, leaves torn off stems
* salt & pepper

For pasta:
* 1 cup pesto sauce
* 250 g (8 oz) pasta of your choice
* 2 green zucchinis
* 2 yellow squash
* 1 lemon, zested into strips & juiced
* chili flakes
* salt & pepper

How to make pesto sauce:

1 Make sure you process in this order; if you put the basil in too early, it turns brown! In the blender, process the garlic, nuts and cheese first, then add a little oil, some mint, parsley and coriander, some more oil and then the torn basil leaves.

2 Season blended mixture at the end, when you can tell how much salt or pepper to use based on the saltiness of the cheese and the peppery mint. Add more or less olive oil to taste and consistency – sometimes it varies depending on how much moisture all the ingredients have. The parsley helps keep it green.

3 Place pesto in a Tupperware container, pour over a little more olive oil to seal the mix from the air, and put the lid on tight! This will keep in the fridge for 5 days.

How to make pesto pasta:

1 Cook the pasta according to the packet directions. Drain and place in a serving bowl. Toss with the pesto sauce. Cover loosely to keep warm.

2 Grate zucchinis and yellow squash on the medium-sized holes straight into the serving bowl. Add the lemon juice and zest, chili flakes and salt & pepper to taste.

3 Garnish with shaved Parmesan and some torn basil and mint leaves.

Pesto sauce on toast topped with sliced tomato is one of life's delicacies. Use a dollop of pesto as a base for a salad dressing. Pesto rocks.

Hot Tips

Eggplant, mushrooms, seafood and chicken can be added or substituted.
Keep the following handy for the garnish: grated or shaved Parmesan, torn basil leaves, toasted pine nuts or breadcrumbs.

Hot tips!

Put some risotto on a plate and tip it at an angle to test the consistency. If it moves slowly across the plate like a lava flow, it is perfect!

As with the Pumpkin Soup recipe on page 160, you can try these great substitutes: leeks for onion; butternut squash for pumpkin, chicken stock for vegetable stock; normal thyme or parsley for lemon thyme.

At a pinch - i.e. it's raining and you just got home and you forgot to get the Arborio rice! - you can use another short-grain rice instead. We recommend the extra effort to get the Arborio rice.

Pumpkin Risotto

Rice dishes are so great for energy and risotto is a classic. A really easy dish, risotto is quite peaceful to make. Whether you find yourself cooking for yourself or a dinner party, risotto is another mainstay that will keep you and your flatmates happy! We find ourselves meditating to an almost zen-like state while we make this dish, which makes the cooking time fly by ... it's all in the stirring! Serves: 4 people

Tools:

knife & cutting board
baking dish (sheet), metal spoon
2 medium saucepans
wooden spoon or ladle

Shopping list:

* 1 pumpkin (butternut squash), about 1 kg (2 lb)
* 2 tablespoons olive oil
* 4 sprigs fresh lemon thyme
* salt & pepper
* 4 cups (32 fl oz) vegetable stock
* 1 white onion, chopped
* 2 cloves garlic, crushed
* 1 cup (7 oz) Arborio rice (Italian rice for risotto)
* 1 wedge Parmesan cheese, for grating

How to make it:

1 Preheat oven to 200°C (400°F). Peel pumpkin and scoop out seeds.

2 Dice pumpkin into 3 cm (1¼ inch) cubes and coat with some olive oil, sprigs of the thyme and salt & pepper by tossing in a bowl.

3 Place pumpkin on the baking dish (sheet) and roast in the oven for about 30 minutes or until tender and slightly caramelized/golden. Keep warm by covering with aluminum foil.

4 Heat up the stock in a saucepan and keep on a low flame.

5 Sautee together the onion and garlic in olive oil until translucent and slightly sizzling.

6 Put the Arborio rice in the saucepan and stir rapidly to coat with the olive oil. Keep stirring so that the grains go glossy and almost seem to stick to the saucepan.

7 Add one ladle of the stock to the rice – that hiss is a famous part of the risotto making, indicating that the rice is absorbing the flavor and will plump up beautifully.

8 Stir gently but with purpose! Continue to ladle stock in bit by bit, as it is absorbed. At about the 20 minute mark, add the diced pumpkin and stir through.

9 Test the rice – if it is soft but still a bit firm, add more warm stock, or water if needed.

10 Grate or shave the Parmesan and add in to the mix. Adjust the seasonings, adding more liquid if necessary. A risotto should be moist, not dry.

Tempeh & Brown Rice Stir-fry

This is one of our favorite "big bowl" comfort food dishes. Good for you, full of flavor and very easy to prepare. Serves: 2 people

Tools:

knife & cutting board
medium saucepan
wok
grater, wooden spoons

Shopping list:

- 250 g (8 oz) mushrooms
- 1 packet tempeh, any flavor
- 1 supermarket bag spinach
- 1 tablespoon vegetable oil
- 1 "thumb"-sized piece of ginger, peeled & grated
- 1 clove garlic, minced
- 1 bunch green onions, cleaned & chopped all the way to the green
- 1 cup (7 oz) organic brown rice, cooked according to the packet directions & kept warm
- $1/3$ cup (3 fl oz) Tamari
- 1 lemon, juiced
- 1 tablespoon toasted sesame seeds

How to make it:

1 Slice the mushrooms to about 2 cm ($3/4$ inch) thick. Cube the tempeh to be about 2 cm ($3/4$ inch) square.

2 Clean and pick over the spinach leaves – you can leave the stalks on even if they are long as they are good for you too!

3 Heat the oil on medium heat and add the ginger, garlic and when they become fragrant, add the mushrooms, then the green onion and rice.

4 Turn the heat up to high, and add the tempeh and then the spinach. Working quickly, pour in the Tamari and the lemon juice, shaking the pan with your wrist to get the vegetables and rice moving around and mixing.

5 Tip into two bowls and garnish with the sesame seeds.

For the mushrooms: any type works, but we love shiitake or button mushrooms

168

Tempeh is a staple for those who don't eat meat. It comes in a variety of textures and flavors at your local health food store or good grocer.

169

try this!

Other great substitutions:
Tofu for tempeh
Eggplant for mushroom
Any onion for the green onion
Any nuts for the sesame seeds
Rice noodles for the rice

try this!

Serve with an organic brown basmati, **curry sides [page 154]** and naan bread, Turkish bread, chapattis or pappadums.

You can **substitute with any vegetable**. The only rule with curries is that you should cook the harder vegetables first and put the softer ones in later so that they retain their shape and consistency.

We use store-bought **mild curry paste** – a time saver and something that you can have in your pantry or in your fridge as it keeps for quite a while. If you want your curry **super hot**, use a curry paste that specifies the degree of intensity - it's up to you. Burn baby burn!

Put on a **Bollywood movie** and throw a few **Indian cushions** around for a casual and fun dinner at home.

170

Vegetable & Cashew Curry

A great staple for any night in or quick dinner party – the variety for this is limited only by your imagination and the vegetables available either in your fridge already or at the market!

Serves: 4 hungry people

Tools:

knife & cutting board
medium saucepan
mixing bowl
grater, wooden spoons

Shopping list:

* 1 tablespoon vegetable oil
* 1 onion, sliced chunky
* 3 stalks celery, sliced chunky
* 1 "thumb"-sized piece of ginger, peeled & grated
* 4 tablespoons mild curry paste
* 1 cup (5 oz) each of the following vegetables, diced to the same size: pumpkin (butternut squash), sweet potato, carrots, eggplant, cauliflower, zucchini
* 400 g (13 oz) can diced tomatoes
* 1 cup (6 oz) canned chickpeas, drained & rinsed
* 4 cups (32 fl oz) vegetable or chicken stock, or water
* $1/2$ cup (3 oz) golden raisins
* 1 cup ($5^1/3$ oz) unsalted roasted cashews

How to make it:

1 In a large pot, add vegetable oil, onion, celery and ginger and allow to simmer. Add curry paste and stir to coat vegetables.

2 When you can smell the aroma of the curry, add the hard vegetables you have prepared, and then add the tomatoes. Add the chickpeas, then the eggplants, stirring gently to make sure that they all get coated with the paste. Cook gently on medium heat for 5 minutes.

3 Start adding the vegetable stock – the first cup or two should bring the volume of the liquid slightly above the vegetables. Turn the flame to low and let simmer. Check every 15 minutes to add stock as needed and stir.

4 At end of the first 30 minutes, add the soft vegetables – like the cauliflower, zucchinis or any other vegetable you've added, such as capsicums (bell peppers).

5 Add the raisins. Taste and adjust seasonings such as salt – if you want a stronger curry flavor, add more paste. If you are out of stock at this point, just add water as needed.

6 This curry can simmer gently for hours. The longer and more gently it cooks, the better the flavor. Stir the cashews through the curry just before serving.

This is a dish that tastes better on the second or third day as the flavors really soak in more deeply.

171

Ezy-goan Prawn Curry

Take a trip to southern India with girlo's super-easy curry - one of the quickest you can make. Prawns (shrimp) don't need a lot of cooking, so it's a fast ride ... Serves 2 people

Tools:
knife & cutting board
medium saucepan
grater, wooden spoons

Shopping list:
* 1 cup (7 oz) organic basmati or jasmine rice, cooked according to the packet directions & kept warm
* 1 tablespoon vegetable oil
* 1 "thumb"-sized piece of ginger, peeled & grated
* 1 clove garlic, minced
* 1 white onion, sliced thinly
* 1 standard jar mild Indian curry paste
* 2 x 400 ml (13 fl oz) cans light coconut milk
* 500 g (16 oz) green king prawns (jumbo shrimp), peeled but with the tail left on
* $1/4$ bunch fresh coriander (cilantro)
* 1 lime, quartered

How to make it:

1 In the saucepan, add the oil and saute the ginger, garlic and onion. Add about 3 tablespoons of the curry paste you have chosen, and let it simmer gently on the heat until it becomes fragrant.

2 Add the coconut milk and bring to a gentle bubble. Squeeze one of the lime quarters into the liquid - then drop it in to flavor the curry.

3 Drop the prawns into the liquid and let them poach on a medium heat. Do not boil, or you will overcook the prawns. They will only need about 8-10 minutes on medium-low heat.

4 Get the bowls ready by scooping in the rice and then ladling the prawn curry over the top. It will almost be a soup!

5 Garnish with the sprigs of coriander and the remaining lime quarters. Serve with Indian breads and tomato pickle (page 146).

173

Hot tips:
Substitute other
seafood - try **mussels**,
big chunks of firm-
fleshed fish like **tuna**,
swordfish or halibut.

We prefer to use light coconut
milk but if you prefer a
richer tasting recipe the
full-cream milk will work just
as well.

You can use a mild curry or
a really hot one for this
recipe - you choose!

Keep stock of
mixed beans in
your pantry as a
time saver.

Tunisian Tuna & Bean Salad

We just love a salad that is totally filling and at the same time leaves you wanting more! We looked to Tunisia for inspiration and the result is this fave mean bean and green recipe. Serves: 2 people

Tools:

knife & cutting board
strainer
mixing bowls, wooden spoon
griller (broiler) pan or barbecue

Ingredients:

For the salad base:
* ¼ bunch fresh mint leaves only
* ¼ bunch fresh dill, picked off the stem
* 1 supermarket bag of baby spinach leaves
* 400 g (13 oz) can mixed beans, drained & rinsed
* ½ punnet (tub) each red and yellow cherry tomatoes, cut in half
* 1 small red onion, diced
* 1 continental (telegraph) cucumber, washed, seeded & diced, skin on
* 60 g (2 oz) fresh mung beans

For the dressing:
* 3 tablespoons olive oil
* 1 tablespoon red wine vinegar
* 1 teaspoon Dijon mustard
* salt & pepper

For the tuna:
* 2 teaspoons turmeric
* 1 tablespoon lemon juice
* 1 garlic clove, minced
* 1 tablespoon curry powder
* 1 tablespoon olive oil
* salt & pepper
* 2 x 180 g (6 oz) center-cut tuna fillets
* 2 lemon wedges

How to make the salad:

Assemble the ingredients on each serving plate in layers with the leaves first, then the beans and vegetables tossed together. Cover and keep in the fridge until you're ready to cook and serve the tuna. Mix all the dressing ingredients in a small jar and keep handy.

How to make the tuna:

1 Mix together spices, oils and seasonings. Smear paste over tuna and turn to coat other side.

2 Heat griller or barbecue until smoking. Spray the griller with non-stick spray oil or wipe some olive oil over it.

3 Cook the tuna on both sides for approximately 2 minutes per side for rare, 4 minutes for well done. We prefer the rare!

4 Cut each fillet into two wedges and place on top of the salad, pour the dressing over and serve with lemon wedges as a garnish.

Hot tips: **Any fish works for this and you can put any vegetables or leaves, such as cos (Romaine) lettuce or field greens, into the salad.** A bottle dressing will also work if that is easier and faster.

The heat of the tuna carries over into the salad and gently warms up the flavors.

Roast Leg O'Lamb on a Bed of Onions

Roast lamb is a classic recipe. You'll never be without room-mates if you can master this one! Serves: approx 4-6 people as dinner, (and there should be enough left over for snacks, sandwiches, salads etc. afterwards)

Tools:

knife & cutting board
medium baking dish (sheet), Pyrex casserole dish or aluminum foil trays

Ingredients:
* 3 tablespoons olive oil
* sea salt & pepper
* 1 lamb leg, approx 1½ kg (3 lb)
* 3 garlic cloves, peeled & thinly sliced
* 4 stalks rosemary, torn into sprigs
* 3 red onions, peeled without cutting

1 Preheat oven to 200°C (400°F). Rub olive oil, salt and pepper into lamb.

2 Make 8-10 holes all over the lamb with the knife, then stuff with the sliced garlic and a sprig of the rosemary.

3 Cut the peeled onions into quarters, lay in the baking dish and drizzle with some of the olive oil.

4 Lay the leg of lamb down on the onions and throw over any leftover garlic or rosemary.

5 Bake for about 1½ hours or until crispy but still very pink. Rest on the serving/carving platter for 10 minutes.

6 Serve with roast potatoes and a simple green salad, with the onions scattered around the lamb.

Hot Tip: You can substitute onions with parsnips, celery hearts, baby carrots, pumpkin pieces, baby onions, French shallots or leeks. The vegies are to your taste and preference.

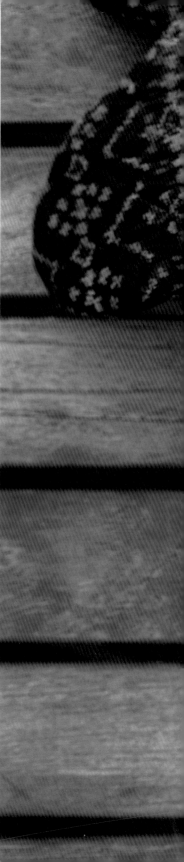

177

Style up a storm, go mad with candles and the Indian or Moroccan theme. Cushions on the floor, put the latest chillout CD in the sound system and you're away!

Barbecued Lamb Rack with Pickled Cucumber Ribbons

This recipe makes use of the fantastic array of condiments available in most supermarkets. Pick up a jar of either Malaysian, Thai, or Indian or (my favorite) Moroccan spice paste and use it as a time saver as well as for that extra flavor ... it's a good old barbie but with a bit of an Asian twist. Serves: 2 people as dinner, 4 if appetizers

Tools:

knife & cutting board
mixing bowl, ceramic or glass
small saucepan
peeler

Shopping list:

* 1 largish garlic clove, peeled & smashed with a knife
* 1 tablespoon olive oil
* sea salt & pepper
* 1 lamb rack with approx 8 cutlets (chops)
* 1 small jar spice paste such as Moroccan spices
* 1 tablespoon mirin (Asian grocery stores and some supermarkets)
* 1 tablespoon rice vinegar
* 1 continental (telegraph) cucumber
* 1 cup (12 oz) honey
* 1/3 bunch fresh mint

How to make it:

1 Preheat griller (broiler) to 200°C (400°F) or heat barbecue grill on high. Rub garlic all over the lamb. Pour over the olive oil and season with salt & pepper. Then smear jar of spice paste onto the fat meaty side of the rack.

2 Rub the griller or barbecue with some olive oil to reduce stickiness, and place rack paste side down to the left of the flames so it cooks by indirect heat.

3 Meanwhile, mix the mirin and rice vinegar together in a small pan, and bring to a gentle boil, then turn off and set aside.

4 Peel the cucumber into ribbons and put into a ceramic or glass bowl. Pour the warm mirin mixture over the top and turn to coat. When cool, tear the fresh mint leaves and sprinkle in.

5 At about the 10 minute mark, turn the rack over and cook for a further 8 minutes. Bring the rack out, cover with aluminum foil and rest for 5 minutes. This allows the juices to settle and the heat to carry over. Cook the rack just a little bit more. This should bring the rack to about rare to medium rare.

6 Drizzle the honey over the top of the lamb, and serve with a side of the pickled cucumber ribbons.

Tamari Glazed Chicken

This can be prepared the day before you need to cook it. The flavor deepens the longer it marinates. If you have any left over, it makes a wonderful snack on its own or thrown into a bowl of miso soup. Serves: 4-6 people

Tools:

knife & cutting board
measuring jug (pitcher)
mixing bowl
roasting/baking dish (sheet) or
aluminum foil tray
serving platter

Shopping list:

For the marinade:

* 1 cup (8 fl oz) Tamari or soy sauce
* 1/3-1 teaspoon chili powder (depending on your taste)
* 1/4 cup (2 fl oz) sesame oil
* 1/3 cup (3 fl oz) mirin
* 2 tablespoons sugar
* 1 clove garlic, peeled
* salt, to taste

For the chicken:

* 1 1/2 kg (3 lb) organic whole chicken, or 6 chicken breasts, bone & skin on
* 3 tablespoons toasted sesame seeds
* 1 bunch green onions, sliced on the diagonal "oriental cut" style

How to make it:

1 Preheat oven to 200°C (400°F). Clean and prepare chicken by giving it a quick rinse inside and out and patting dry thoroughly with paper towels. Cut the chicken in half along the backbone and then into quarters. Lay out in a roasting/baking dish (sheet) wiped with some oil or sprayed with non-stick oil spray. If using the individual breasts, clean and lay out in dish in the same manner.

2 To make the marinade: Mix together the Tamari, chili powder, sesame oil, mirin, sugar until combined. Crush or slice the garlic finely with some salt and add to marinade. Pour over chicken pieces. Set aside in the fridge for about 1 hour turning a couple of times. (You can prepare the day before up to this point and marinate overnight.)

3 Roast in the oven uncovered for 45-50 minutes, turning and basting (spooning the marinade over chicken) each 15 minutes. If using the pieces, your cooking time will be about 25-30 minutes. The best way to tell if chicken is done is to pierce the skin and if the juices that flow out are clear, it's ready to eat.

4 Lay out pieces on your serving platter, spoon some more of the marinade - now "sauce" - over. Be generous!

5 Garnish with the toasted sesame seeds and sliced green onions.

Serve with steamed rice and seaweed "Japanese-style" (ohitashi).

Hot tip:
At step 4, you can prick the skins of the chicken pieces and sear in a hot frying pan with 2 tablespoons of oil to get that crispy caramelized look. Afterwards, place back in the roasting dish and continue to cook in the oven. This is an optional step.

Portuguese Grilled Chicken

Sun, beach, barbecue, chicken ... the easiest summer meal. Do this ahead of the time you need it so it can be ready for snacks, a no-fuss dinner or for that beach picnic. We like to use organic chicken because it has great flavor and we know it is safe. Serves: 6 people

Tools:
knife & cutting board
mixing bowl

Shopping list:
* ⅓ cup (3 fl oz) olive oil
* sea salt & pepper
* 2 tablespoons smoked or plain paprika
* ½ tablespoon chili powder
* 2 tablespoons castor (superfine) sugar
* 2 lemons, grated for zest & juiced
* 1 bunch fresh oregano, finely chopped
* 3 cloves garlic, crushed
* 6 chicken breasts, bone & skin on

How to make it:

1 Preheat griller (broiler) or barbecue on high. Toss all ingredients except chicken together in a bowl and stir well to combine.

2 Place chicken in a roasting/baking dish (sheet) and coat with marinade mixture, setting aside in the fridge for 1 hour (or overnight), turning chicken to coat frequently. Let rest at room temperature for 10 minutes before cooking.

3 Brush griller (broiler) with oil, then place chicken on griller breast skin side down. Don't touch for 8 minutes! Lower the heat if necessary due to flames and smoking.

4 Turn chicken onto bone side and let cook for another 12 minutes. Pull off grill and let rest for 2 minutes. When pierced with a knife, the juices should run clear.

5 Plate up and serve with roast potatoes or carrots and a green side salad.

Hot tips!

If you are using boneless/skinless chicken breasts, your cooking time will be a little less, about 15 minutes all up including resting time. However, all grillers and ovens vary, so make sure the juices are nice and clear or that the internal meat temperature is over 145°C (280°F) with a thermometer. However, **it's best to get the chicken with the bone on,** because the bones are what help to keep it juicy.

Once the food's ready, set up your beach towels or blankets and kick back.

Autumn Roast Vegetables

Vegetarians will love this dish as it is, but it also goes well with summer barbecue meats. We love it around a good old-fashioned roast too! This may be the dinner you cook on weekends away or to surprise a family member for a special birthday dinner. Nice one. Serves: 6-8 people

Tools:
knife & cutting board
mixing bowl
medium roasting/baking dish
(sheet), aluminum foil tray or
Pyrex casserole dish

Shopping list:
* 250 g (8 oz) parsnips
* 250 g (8 oz) pumpkin
  (butternut squash)
* 250 g (8 oz) turnips or red
  onions
* 250 g (8 oz) sweet potatoes or
  garnet yams
* 125 g (4 oz) green onion
  bulbs, trimmed to the bulb
  plus 10 cm (4 inches) of stalk
* 125 g (4 oz) baby squash
  (pattypan)
* 250 g (8 oz) baby capsicums
  (bell peppers)
* 125 g (4 oz) baby eggplants
* 1/4 cup (2 fl oz) olive oil
* sea salt flakes & cracked
  pepper
* half bunch fresh thyme
* 2 tablespoons Italian (flat
  leaf) parsley, chopped

How to make it:

1 Preheat the oven to 180°C (350°F). Clean and scrub all the vegetables, peel if necessary (e.g. parsnips).

2 Toss in the mixing bowl with the olive oil, seasonings and fresh herbs.

3 Place all of the hard vegetables first into the roasting/baking dish (sheet) spread in a single layer and cook for about 25 minutes.

4 Next add in the soft vegetables for another 25 minutes of cooking. Serve in roasting/baking dish or serve onto individual plates.

The best thing about this dish is that you can **puree any leftover vegies into a soup** or put them cold into a salad with a vinaigrette dressing.

Note to girlo chefs: This dish takes an hour to cook plus preparation time (how fast can you peel vegies?) so, if you've got people coming, don't leave it to the last minute!

Hot tips!

This shopping list is only a suggestion - add or substitute any vegetables you may prefer. Be creative with it!

We like to use Maldon sea salt, which is a well-known brand with a nice texture, but any sea salt flakes will work just as well.

Classic "Roastie" Potatoes with Lemon Salt

Who doesn't love roasted potatoes - hot or cold? They go with just about everything, and the leftovers make a great potato salad. There are so many varieties of potatoes available so you can choose the ones you like best. Go for whatever roasts well ... are you a skin-on or skin-off kind of girl?

Serves: 6 people

Tools:
knife & cutting board
mixing bowl
medium roasting/baking dish (sheet) or Pyrex casserole dish

Shopping list:
* 500 g (16 oz) fingerling or red desiree potatoes
* 1/3 cup (3 fl oz) olive oil
* sea salt & pepper
* 1 tablespoon finely grated lemon zest

How to make it:

1 Preheat oven to 200°C (400°F). Halve the potatoes and toss them in the olive oil, salt, pepper and lemon zest in a bowl. Mix thoroughly.

2 Place in a roasting/baking dish (sheet) cut side up. Roast on the lower rack of the oven for the first 20 minutes.

3 Move to the top rack of the oven for maximum crispiness; they are done when they become puffed and golden.

4 Toss with a little lemon zest and more sea salt & pepper while hot, then serve!

Keep some of the lemon zest for the garnish.

Vegetable Crisp

This is a stand-alone dish or a largish side dish for a roast dinner. Serves: approx 4 people

Tools:
measure cups/spoons
knife & cutting board
grater
small mixing bowl
medium roasting/baking dish
(sheet) or Pyrex casserole dish

Shopping list:
* 4 zucchinis
* 4 yellow squash
* 1 large Italian eggplant
* 1 red onion
* 1 cup (4 oz) packet breadcrumbs
* $1/4$ cup (1 oz) grated fresh Parmesan
* 1 tablespoon of chopped fresh Italian (flat leaf) parsley, oregano, basil, lemon thyme sea salt & pepper
* 1 garlic clove, peeled & smashed with a knife
* 400 g (13 oz) can crushed tomatoes
* $1/2$ cup (4 fl oz) olive oil

How to make it:

1 Preheat oven to 180°C (350°F). Slice the zucchini and squash into 2 cm (³/₄ inch) thick rounds. Slice the eggplant into 1.5 cm (¹/₂ inch) thick wedges. Cut the onions into medium-sized quarters.

2 Mix together the breadcrumbs, Parmesan, herbs and season with salt & pepper.

3 Wipe out the roasting/baking dish (sheet) with olive oil and run the smashed garlic clove around the inside to give it extra flavor. Discard.

4 Toss the crushed tomatoes with ¹/₄ cup (2 fl oz) olive oil, salt, pepper and half the chopped herbs, and toss the sliced vegetables through to coat.

5 Lay out the vegetables in alternating layers overlapping like the shingles on a roof. Drizzle the remaining olive oil over the top.

6 Spread the breadcrumb mix over the top, and let sit for 1 hour in a cool place while the flavors blend together.

7 Bake in the oven, covered for 45 minutes, then put under the griller (broiler) for a brief time to crisp up the breadcrumb mix, about 3 minutes. Keep a close eye so that it doesn't burn - we said vegetable crisp not charred!

Hot tip:
You can prepare this the night before – just don't cook it until 30 minutes before you are ready to eat!

Roasted Tomatoes

Great in the summer, especially if you can get your hands on some home-grown tomatoes. These will keep in the fridge, covered in a Tupperware container or the like, for about 4 days. Serves: approx 4-6 as part of a buffet or with a breakfast of scrambled eggs and grilled bread

Tools:
knife & cutting board
mixing bowl
medium roasting/baking dish (sheet) or Pyrex casserole dish

Ingredients:
* $1/2$ cup (4 fl oz) olive oil
* 1 bunch lemon thyme
* 1 bunch oregano, chopped
* 2 tablespoons castor (superfine) sugar
* 2 tablespoons balsamic vinegar
* sea salt & pepper
* 4 peeled garlic cloves, smashed with a knife
* 1 punnet (tub) yellow pear cherry tomatoes
* 1 punnet (tub) red pear cherry tomatoes
* 250 g (8 oz) red plum tomatoes
* 250 g (8 oz) yellow beefsteak tomatoes

How to make it:

1 Preheat oven to 150°C (300°F). Mix the olive oil, herbs, sugar and salt & pepper in a bowl with the balsamic vinegar. Mix to combine lightly.

2 Wash and gently dry the tomatoes. Cut the plum and the beefsteak tomatoes in half and gently squeeze out excess liquid. (You can save this liquid and use it in the Vegetable Crisp on page 180. The fresh tomato juice keeps for 3 days in the fridge.)

3 Toss the tomatoes through the olive oil mix. Wipe roasting/baking dish (sheet) with oil then wipe over with garlic clove. Discard. Arrange tomatoes in the dish.

4 Bake slowly for about 1 hour or until nicely caramelized. If doing overnight, make sure oven is on the lowest setting. Serve warm or cold!

If you still have some left over, blend with chicken or vegetable stock for an easy tomato soup.

Hot tip:
If you are baking this dish slowly overnight on the lowest setting on your oven, leave a big note for yourself somewhere (on the bathroom door or inside the fridge on the milk perhaps!) so you don't forget about them!

191

Vanilla Ice Cream with Berry Swirl & Topping

For girlo scouts who like to be prepared, this is a great do-ahead dessert. It incorporates some pre-made ingredients with a special home-made sauce. Serves: 3-4 people

Tools:
measure cups/spoons
3 small saucepans/pans
mixing bowl
jelly mould, loaf tin or freezer-safe glass bowl (e.g. Pyrex)
plastic wrap

Shopping list:
* 1 tub (about 16 fl oz) of the best vanilla ice cream in your supermarket!
* 1 punnet (tub) blackberries
* 1 punnet (tub) raspberries
* 1 punnet (tub) strawberries
* 1 cup (7 oz) castor (superfine) sugar
* juice of 1 lemon
* water, as needed

How to make it:

1 Let ice cream soften on your bench while you prepare the swirl and sauce.

2 Take a few berries of each type and set aside for garnish. Spread the three types of berries equally in the three saucepans and add $1/3$ cup ($2 1/3$ oz) of sugar, $1/3$ of the lemon juice and about a tablespoon of water to each saucepan. Cook until fruit has broken down. Cool each of the sauces and allow them to thicken.

3 Turn the ice cream out into a mixing bowl. Stir half of each of the cooled sauces through, and swirl with a wooden spoon until nicely blended. Don't over-blend - keep the swirl effect.

4 Line the mould with plastic wrap and put the ice cream into the mould. Cover with more plastic wrap and place carefully in the freezer overnight. Reserve the leftover sauces for serving.

5 When ready to serve, take the ice cream out of the mould and slice onto plates or simply scoop out with an ice cream scooper. Heat up the sauces, in small pans. Pour over the ice cream and garnish with the reserved berries. Serve immediately.

It's best served when slightly melting.

193

Cool tip:
If you're going to have
ice cream, look for
the natural ingredient
versions, which use
full cream. If you're
going to go the
non-dairy version,
look for frozen soy or
goat's milk yogurt as a
substitute.

Lychee Slushy

A quick-and-easy dessert or afternoon snack. Lychees make a refreshing change but other fruit slushies work just as well. Be creative! Serves: 2 people

Tools:

can opener
blender
serving bowls

Shopping list:

* 400 g (13 oz) can lychees in syrup
* fresh mint

How to make it:

1 The night before you wish to eat this, empty contents of the can into a durable plastic or zip-lock bag or Tupperware freezer container. Seal tightly and place in freezer.

2 24 hours later, remove from freezer 10 minutes before churning so it has a chance to soften.

3 Place in the blender and whiz quickly in spurts. You may need to use a wooden spoon (when stopping the blender naturally!) to quickly mix the chunks if the blender isn't getting through them.

4 Scoop out into your serving bowls and garnish with fresh mint.

Substitute other canned or fresh fruit and do the same thing!

Hot tip: Serve in vintage-style glass bowls (check out your local op shop) and style up with oriental-inspired trays, napkins and music – go China girl!

NOT MOTHER HUBBARD'S CUPBOARD

It is a brave new world indeed when you live by yourself. Ditto if your parents have gone away and all of a sudden you have to do the shopping and cook the meals too. An upside of this is the masses of respect you'll gain for what your parents have done for you (and done for many years at that!). Planning what to buy on a weekly basis (and within a certain budget) is one life skill you will continue to revise throughout your life. What follows is a very basic starting point for your cupboard and fridge. You may not live away from home yet, but you can guarantee it will be helpful for when you do – even for when you are going away for a weekend.

Cupboard staples:
- rolled oats
- brown rice (short grain)
- white rice (long grain or jasmine)
- pasta
- rice noodles (thick and thin)
- wholemeal (wholewheat)/ unbleached flour
- raw sugar
- honey
- peanut butter
- maple syrup
- rice crackers
- crispbread
- taco shells
- corn chips
- tea biscuits
- vegetable or chicken stock (liquid)

Bread:
- pita or mountain bread (roll-ups)
- sourdough
- sliced spelt bread

Canned food:
- coconut milk (light)
- tomatoes
- chickpeas
- baby corn
- tuna
- salmon
- baked beans
- red kidney beans
- cannellini beans
- tea (green, herbal, black)

Cooking aids and condiments:
- sea salt flakes
- black pepper
- Chili flakes
- soy sauce (Tamari)
- balsamic vinegar
- white wine vinegar
- olive oil
- wasabi paste
- curry paste
- sundried tomatoes
- sesame seeds
- baking soda
- baking powder
- vanilla essence

Nuts:
- pine nuts
- pepitas
- raw almonds
- plain cashews

Green vegetables:
- broccoli
- rocket (arugula)
- lettuce (variety)
- green onions
- bok choy (Chinese chard)
- spinach (baby/ large leaf)

Vegetables:
- garlic
- celery
- mushrooms (brown, shiitake, white)
- carrots
- capsicums (bell peppers), red, green, yellow
- tomatoes (vine ripened and baby)
- cabbage (red or green)
- potatoes
- pumpkin (butternut squash)
- red onion

Fridge stuff:
- milk (organic)
- soy milk
- rice milk
- yogurt (organic, soy, sheep or goat's)
- cheese (hard yellow, goat's)
- butter (no-salt, olive oil)
- eggs
- tofu
- tempeh

Fruit:
- apples (red/ green)
- oranges (navel)
- bananas
- avocado
- strawberries
- seasonal fruit

Handy tools for the kitchen:
- sieve
- colander (which easily doubles as a steamer above a saucepan!)
- grater
- measuring spoons and cups
- good cutting board
- good sharp knives in varying sizes
- 3-4 different-sized saucepans
- a small and large frying pan
- wok

This list is not exhaustive – it is a basic list. It's a handy one to keep with you when you go grocery shopping, just to remind you of what may need replacing.

Just because measuring stuff can be a bit tricky until you get really used to it (especially for baking where it's a bit more crucial than for other types of cooking) we have come up with a chart to help. The chart also takes into account our girlo chefs on both sides of the international dateline, just so no one misses out. Whether you prefer metric or not, you can cook in any place and have food emerge perfectly. Here is a basic chart:

Grams (g)	Weight/ounces (oz)
30 g	1 oz
60 g	2 oz
250 g	8 oz (1/2 lb)
500 g	16 oz (1 lb)
1 kilogram (kg)	32 oz (2 lb)

Some measuring rule of thumb notes – because sugar and rice (and other ingredients) aren't always equal!

	Grams	Ounces	Cup
Coconut	30 g	1 oz	1/3
Rice	100 g	3 1/2 oz	1/2
Sugar	110 g	3 1/2 oz	1/3
Yogurt	130 g	4 oz	1/2
Sultanas	90 g	3 oz	1/2
Flour	75 g	2 1/2 oz	1/3

Milliliters	Teaspoon
1.25 ml	–
2.5 ml	–
5 ml	1
10 ml	2
20 ml	1 tablespoon (4 teaspoons)

Liters	Cup	Fluid ounces (fl oz)
60 ml	1/4	2
80 ml	1/3	2 1/2
125 ml	1/2	4
180 ml	3/4	6
250 ml	1	8
500 ml	2	16
750 ml	3	24
1 Liter	4	32

Here are a few general things for all girlo chefs to keep in mind while using the recipes in the book:

• Oven temperatures are in Celsius (ºC) and Fahrenheit (ºF).

• Sea salt flakes are our preferred salt for recipes. We use the Maldon brand – but ask your local delicatessen or gourmet food provider for a brand that they stock.

• Tupperware is one brand of airtight containers – there are many others available. Check your local supermarket or kitchen wares store.

• Our standard "cup" that we refer to in the recipes is the same as 250 ml or 8 fl oz. We stress though that you could quite easily use a normal kitchen tea cup and the proportions would still work.

Further reading for Girlosophers

Whether it's the effects of carbohydrates on energy levels, global corporate behavior, body image, women's health issues or the karmic effects of eating animal products you are interested in, here is a list of my recommended reading. Girlosophers interested in finding out more in the areas of health and nutrition and the mind-body-spirit effects of how and what we eat will find the books below helpful and enlightening.

Jennie Brand-Miller et al., **The New Glucose Revolution,** Hodder Headline, 2002

Dr Kathleen DesMaisons, **Potatoes not Prozac,** Simon & Shuster, 1998

Leslie Kenton, **The Raw Energy Bible,** Vermilion, Random House, 2001

Naomi Klein, **No Logo,** Flamingo, Harper Collins, 2001

Dr Christiane Northrup, **Women's Bodies, Women's Wisdom,** Judy Piatkus (Publishers) Ltd, 1995

Ruth Ozeki, **My Year of Meat,** Picador, Pan Macmillan Publishers, 2003

Janella Purcell's **Elixir,** Allen & Unwin, 2004

Sogyal Rinpoche, **The Tibetan Book of Living and Dying,** Harper Collins, San Francisco, 1992

Rosemary Stanton, **Eating for Peak Performance,** Allen & Unwin, 1994

Mark Wahlqvist, **Food and Nutrition,** 2nd edition, Allen & Unwin, 2002

Naomi Wolf, **The Beauty Myth,** Vintage Books, 1991

198

Credits

OUR GIRLO SUPER CHEF: Kate Paul

Kate Paul has cooked and eaten her way around the world for 15 years and in that time she has prepared meals for just about everyone in showbiz, including The Rolling Stones, Tina Turner, The Spice Girls and Robbie Williams. Kate survived cooking for the Osbournes during their MTV series - she even taught Ozzie how to stuff a turkey! Kate's motto has always been: start fresh, cook with love and eat all in moderation! Kate now runs Food Ink Catering cooking for celebrities and lives in Los Angeles with her husband Mike and their rescued terrier Donald.

Many thanks to Kate for the stunning recipes and for flying so far to cook them for us. And thanks also to the great girlo photographers Amanda McLauchlan and Susi Stitt.

Kate

Amanda

Justine

Anthea

Susi

girlosophy is a proud supporter of War Child
International, the humanitarian aid agency
assisting children in war zones around the
world.

Children are the most innocent victims of
armed conflict. Help the next generation for a
better, more peaceful planet. Please log on to
www.warchild.org.au to see how you can help.

girlosophy is also a proud supporter of the
Tibetan Friendship Group (TFG), a humanitarian
orgnization assisting and rehabilitating
Tibetan refugees in India. His Holiness, Dalai
Lama, the Tibetan spiritual leader, is the
patron of TFG. Please support this worthy
cause. Help TFG restore and preserve the
ancient and gentle culture of Tibet. Visit
www.tibetan.org.au to send a donation or to
see how you can help.

www.girlosophy.com